THE
CALIFORNIA WESTERN
"SKUNK" RAILROAD

by Spencer Crump

ZETA PUBLISHERS COMPANY

Dedicated to
Cynthia Fink Walker Crump
Student, Friend, Wife

The California Western "Skunk" Railroad
By Spencer Crump

Revised Fourth Edition
Art Direction: Victoria Crump McCarthy

Library of Congress Card No.: 98-060224
ISBN: 0-918376-12-2
© 1991, 1992, 1994, 1998 by Spencer Crump
Published by The California Western Railroad
Foot of Laurel Street, P. O. Box 907
Fort Bragg, California 95437
In Cooperation with Zeta Publishers Company

Cover Photograph by the Author: "All Aboard for the Redwood Route!" With Locomotive Engineer Jerry Brooks in the cab, The California Western Super Skunk prepares to leave the depot at Fort Bragg in 1988. Locomotive 45 was making its first trip after being overhauled.

ACKNOWLEDGMENTS

The author expresses his appreciation to those who assisted in preparing this book. They include Gary Milliman and Lynn Hakin, president and chief operating officer respectively of the California Western; Al Arreguin, Henry Foltz, John D. Pacheco, Jill Peterson, and Ray A. Regalia, all of whom are or have been associated with the CWR. In addition he thanks the CWR employees and the people of Fort Bragg, Willits, and the Mendocino Coast for always being so friendly and helpful.

Others assisting were his son, John S. Crump, production director; my wife and friend, Cynthia Walker-Crump, editorial consultant; and my friend, Hank Johnston, for helping with details of the original production. The engineering drawings of Skunk Bus M-80 were made available by the builder, Mack Trucks, Inc. The author thanks his mother, Mrs. Jessie Person Crump, for help with the original manuscript.

Portions of this book were adapted from *Redwoods, Iron Horses, and the Pacific: The Story of the California Western "Skunk" Railroad*, by Spencer Crump: © 1963, 1965, 1971, 1975, 1998 by Spencer Crump.

Printed & Bound in the United States of America

Passengers alight from the Super Skunk at Fort Bragg after the trip from Willits in this photograph, made in 1965 soon after the new steam service was inaugurated. (CWR Photograph by Ed Freitas)

"All Aboard!"

This is the call from the conductor that signals the start of your trip on the California Western "Skunk" Railroad, the happy and scenic journey that takes you from the Pacific Ocean deep into the redwoods.

Indeed, The Redwood Route from the Pacific Ocean at Fort Bragg over spectacular mountains and through ageless redwoods to Willits is as inspiring today as it was when the line was started more than a century ago.

Most American railroads face declining passenger volume. The California Western, however, attracts more people every year to the three-hour trip through towering redwoods that even a Hollywood studio could never duplicate. Many people not acquainted with the CWR think that the short line is a narrow

3

gauge railroad, but it is a standard gauge system. Its builders intended for its cars to be carried from the redwoods to the markets of America, and its passenger coaches once offered through service to and from the San Francisco Bay.

The California Western's winding, climbing route originally had 115 bridges. This led one wit to remark that the railroad must be one long bridge. Landfills and other improvements have reduced the number of bridges to 30 without damaging the scenic beauty. The bears, chipmunks, squirrels, and skunks descended from the animals that watched the railroad being built a century ago still peer from behind trees and shrubs at today's railroad passengers.

This is a history of the California Western Railroad and an account of what you will see when you visit the Mendocino Coast.

Reaching the area is part of the fun. If you travel along Highway 1, you'll enjoy the rugged Mendocino Coast with its beaches, rocks towering from the sea, spectacular cliffs, and picturesque villages. If you drive on U.S. Route 101, you'll see mile upon mile of giant redwood trees plus neat vineyards with their wineries, many of which are open for public tours.

The summer season, stretching from June through September, is the busy time of the year for the area. To be assured of seats on the Skunk railroad, you should contact the California Western office to make ticket reservations. You also should obtain reservations at a motel — many of which post "no vacancy" signs on busy days.

Besides riding over the Redwood Route, you'll want to browse among the shops in the colorful Mendocino towns that have preserved beautiful buildings dating back to the twentieth century. The village of Mendocino, on the coast just south of Fort Bragg, is a picturesque art colony. Much of this atmosphere also is apparent as you stroll through Fort Bragg itself.

When it comes to the train ride, you have a choice of traveling from Fort Bragg to Willits, or from Willits to Fort Bragg. You also can ride the train from either city to Northspur, the station at the middle of the route, and then return to the town from which you started.

The California Western passenger depot is at Laurel Street and Main (Highway 1), just north of Fort Bragg's downtown section. Try to arrive a few minutes early: the station waiting room includes a souvenir shop displaying gifts and other items regarding the railroad and the redwoods.

Rail Bus M-300 is pictured at Ranch soon after joining the California Western roster of equipment in 1963. (CWR Photograph by Ed Freitas)

Locomotive No. 8, built in 1869, paused during a stop in approximately 1910. Trainmen included engineer Ed Hendrickson, conductor Arthur Hanson, and brakeman John Pimentel, all of whom served in operating the first passenger train between Fort Bragg and Willits on December 19, 1911. (CWR)

The depot at Willits is at 229 East Commercial Street, just east of Main Street. It also has a souvenir shop. Built in 1916 of choice clear-grained redwood provided by the Union Lumber Company and two other lumber firms, the depot is one of the most beautiful in America. The town of Willits, established in the late 1870s, was named for Hiram Willits, who in 1857 settled in the area.

Besides riding the Skunk, there is a great deal for visitors to see in both cities. Just a short distance east of the Willits station on Commercial (but on the opposite side of the street) is the Willits Museum. Offering exhibits regarding railroading and the redwoods, the facility is a fascinating place to visit. You also can see many redwood trees on the roads near the city.

At Fort Bragg, there is a museum adjoining the Georgia-Pacific office on Main Street. Another attraction at Fort Bragg is Noyo Harbor, which from the high bridge over Highway 1 looks like a set from a motion picture. The drive down the cliff to the harbor takes you to shops and restaurants specializing in fish dinners. The harbor also is a port for fishermen, of both the sport and commercial varieties.

Fort Bragg itself is like a trip to yesteryear. In 1980, for example, the census gave it a population of 5,019 — an increase of only 424 people in 20 years. While the highways there are improved regularly, the slow growth means that many early-day buildings

5

A variety of locomotives served the California Western during the years. Locomotive No. 5 (above) built by the Hinkley Locomotive Works in 1883, was acquired in 1905 and used until it was scrapped in 1923. Diesel Locomotive 54, built by Baldwin, was scrapped after an accident in 1970. (Both Photographs: CWR)

These loggers called time-out for a photograph while downing a big redwood during the 19th century when there were large stands of the largest trees. Twelve people, including two young women, were able to perch in the undercut of the tree. (California Historical Society) BELOW: Actual-sized reproductions show how much larger are the cones of the inland redwoods (left) than the coastal redwoods (right).

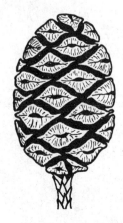

remain and give the city a picturesque atmosphere.

Let's return to the California Western and its redwoods.

California's two distinctively different types of redwoods received their botanical names in 1847 from an Austrian scholar named Stephen Endicher. He designated the genus as sequoia, honoring the developer of the Cherokee alphabet, George Gist, whose Indian name was Sequoya (a different spelling than for the trees).

The variety known as sequoia gigantea flourishes in the Sierra Nevada and the trees are a major attraction in Sequoia National Park. The sequoia sempervirens, popularly called the coastal redwoods, grow along the California coast from just below Carmel north to Oregon. Ranging up to 30 feet in diameter, the inland trees grow up to 300 feet tall and the oldest began growing approximately four thousand years ago. By contrast the coastal redwoods are slimmer, taller, and younger. They are up to 12 feet in diameter, tower as high as 340 feet (taller than a 35-story office building); the oldest began growing approximately two thousand years ago. The wood is less fibrous than that of the inland trees, and therefore is better for building.

The Spanish named the giants palos colorados, a

The Mendocino Coast, with its cliffs, rocks, swift currents, and wildflowers, beckons travelers to the Fort Bragg area. (Photograph by the Author) RIGHT: Trainmen riding an inspection car stopped in the early twentieth century to pose for a picture by a big tree. (CWR)

LEFT: Locomotive No. 21 pulls cars loaded with logs over a bridge on the CWR's Ten Mile River Branch on the coast north of Fort Bragg. This line was discontinued in 1949. ABOVE: These 1907 travelers rode to the point where California Western tracks ended and prepared to board a stagecoach for the next leg of the journey to San Francisco. (CWR)

name that endured when the Americans translated the name literally: redwood trees. The Spanish used the wood, along with adobe brick, for building their famous missions. The Russians, who occupied the northern California coast in the early 1800s, used the timber for constructing Fort Ross, an outpost whose structure endured for more than a century. The reconstructed fort on Highway 1 south of Fort Bragg is preserved as a state historical park.

The discovery of gold at Sutter's Mill triggered an immense boom. Gold from California's Mother Lode and silver from Nevada built San Francisco, but the city by the Golden Gate built its physical self from redwood. Loggers swarmed into the big tree country along the northern California coast and cut the redwoods, some of them two thousand years old. They usually sent milled timber or entire logs southward by sea, for the railroads were not yet built to this isolated and wild area. Indians threatened the loggers, and the army moved in to protect the

workers. One such outpost, established in 1860, was named in honor of Captain Braxton Bragg, a West Point graduate who soon became a major general in the Confederate Army.

Abandoned in 1867, the fort might have been forgotten had not a young man from Wisconsin named Charles Russell Johnson (1859-1940) arrived.

Born in Racine, Wisconsin, Johnson while a boy moved with his family to Michigan. There his father operated saw mills at Saugatuck and St. Ignace, producing an environment that would shape the youth's destiny and subsequently that of the redwood industry. Young Johnson had a bout with illness, and his father sent him west to recuperate. So it was that fourteen-year-old Charles Johnson arrived in San Francisco in 1873. He soon recovered, visited California for eighteen months, and returned home to work in his father's mill. Two years later he left to take a job with the Menominee River Lumber Company in Chicago. There he worked four years,

11

Locomotive No. 4, acquired in 1904, arrived in Fort Bragg by ship. Trainmen and passengers paused for this picture before making a trip into the redwood forest. (CWR)

absorbing countless details regarding production techniques, marketing methods, and the many uses for lumber.

So much had the visit to California impressed young Johnson that in 1881, when twenty-two years old, he returned there to make it his home. While he travelled extensively in California, he failed to find what he wanted until one day a family friend spoke in glowing terms of the big redwoods north of San Francisco. He decided to go there, traveling first by railroad, then by stagecoach, and finally by buckboard over roads which were barely discernible.

When Charles Russell Johnson saw the stately redwoods of the Mendocino Coast, he knew why he decided to make California his home. He fell in love with the redwoods with an affection that would

continue until his death nearly sixty years later.

Among those he met during the journey were Calvin Stewart and James Hunter, veteran loggers in the area of abandoned Fort Bragg. Young Johnson purchased an interest in their holdings, thus establishing the firm of Stewart, Hunter, and Johnson. "C.R.," as friends dubbed the youth, promptly proved his worth as a partner by introducing innovations that revolutionized redwood logging. The partners' logging operations became more efficient after Johnson bought modern machinery he had observed in the Midwest. Mill workers traditionally had worked a single shift; Johnson put operations on a twenty-four hour basis, and the output more than doubled.

By modern standards, logging methods of the era

12

were crude. After being downed by handsaws and axes, hand-operated devices and oxen moved the logs to rivers to be floated to the mills. Moreover, treacherous seas and a lack of harbors along the Mendocino Coast made it difficult for sizeable vessels to serve the mills. Getting the timber to San Francisco, of course, was vital to the economics of the redwood industry. Scanning the area for the most advantageous loading point, "C.R." narrowed the search to the abandoned army post of Fort Bragg, alongside Soldiers Harbor, a sheltered cover large enough for sizeable ships.

Johnson envisioned more than a mere shipping point. He foresaw a city established along with a major mill. Substantial capital would be needed. He therefore organized the Fort Bragg Lumber Company, with funds coming from friends, business associates, and his father. The new organization

Taking time out from building the CWR, these laborers posed for this photograph. One laborer (left) was so eager to continue with the important task that he moved, blurring his image. (CWR)

purchased the assets of Stewart, Hunter, and Johnson, along with additional properties owned by the firm of McPherson and Weatherby on Pudding Creek, Noyo River, and the site of Fort Bragg itself. The first steps were constructing a mill and building a wharf for receiving and shipping.

At ten o'clock on the morning of November 16, 1885, Johnson started a bandsaw — a new invention purchased by a new firm.

The Fort Bragg Lumber Company, forerunner of one of America's great redwood organizations, was in business.

Coincident with formation of the lumber company, Johnson and his fellow investors established a railway, appropriately named the Fort Bragg Railroad. Logging companies in California had used railroads, at least of a primitive nature, as early as 1852. Most railroad logging operations made little, if any, effort to maintain regular schedules or encourage passenger traffic. Logging railroads

Locomotive No. 5 delivers a load of big redwood logs to the wharf at Fort Bragg in the early twentieth century. Many logs were shipped or floated to San Francisco for milling. (CWR)

Conquering the rugged mountains, a steam shovel (above) moves earth to make way for the railroad tracks. BELOW: Laborers clear a slide as they lay rails through the mountains. (Both Photographs: CWR)

ABOVE: This view of early-day construction shows how the abundant timber proved useful in building a CWR right-of-way hugging a mountain. BELOW: Hugging the banks of the Noyo River, the rails of the CWR were pushed into the redwood forest. (Both Photographs: CWR)

In the era of steam, the California Western's locomotives ranked among the best in logging railroads. ABOVE: Locomotive 17, a Baldwin built in 1909, was scrapped in 1938. BELOW: Locomotive 23, also a Baldwin, was built in 1923 and used for nearly 30 years. (Both Photographs: CWR)

LUMBER TRAIN IN FORT BRAGG WOODS

A train pulling lumber and other freight cars approached the camera in this early twentieth century photograph. Trees downed for milling were waiting to be picked up by the tracks. (CWR)

Fort Bragg, 1862.

ABOVE: This sketch shows the way Fort Bragg looked in 1862, a time when the fortress was at its peak of activity. (California Historical Society) BELOW: Locomotive 22, used for 30 years starting in 1921, posed for a photograph soon after its arrival in Fort Bragg. (CWR)

basically were transient, operating only when needed and moved to reach the supply of trees.

The railroad founded by C.R. Johnson became an entirely different type of line. It played an important part not only in the area's industrial life, but also in its social and cultural activities. No other logging railroads in America made the deep impression on American life that was created by the line from Fort Bragg — first by the beauty of its route and later by the distinctiveness of its equipment.

The first locomotive acquired was, in view of the fact that it would be used in the sequoia sempervirens or redwoods, appropriately named Sequoia, also known as Engine No. 1. The unit was a new one built by the Baldwin Locomotive Company, then rated among America's leading producers of railway rolling stock. This showed the importance of the rail line to the lumber company as well as its intentions to develop the system into more than the usual timber operation. Many contemporary logging companies utilized second hand or inferior rail equipment if adequate to haul logs to a loading or milling point. Over the years, the railroad bought and sold locomotives, usually moving into more powerful equipment to serve the growing timber operations. (For a complete list of locomotives, see the roster of equipment at the back of this book).

By 1887 the Fort Bragg Railroad stretched 6.6 miles up Pudding Creek, reaching a point designated as Glen Blair. From here the Glen Blair Lumber Company sent its shipments of redwoods by rail to Fort Bragg, providing the railway company with revenue in addition to that from its parent firm. This year also saw the Fort Bragg Railroad purchase its second locomotive. No. 2, also built by the Baldwin Locomotive Works, was slightly larger than No. 1. Without a doubt the railroad was finding a special place in the hearts of Fort Bragg residents. The company purchased a San Francisco street car and converted it for use as a passenger coach.

What fun!

Business prospered, but the operation required more capital. These funds came with the incorporation on August 17, 1893, of the Union Lumber Company. This firm took over not only the Fort Bragg Lumber Company, but also White and

Railroaders and loggers posed proudly with Locomotive No. 4, pulling a load of logs to the mill, shortly after its purchase in 1904. (CWR)

ABOVE: A train rounds a curved trestle that became renowned with CWR passengers. A dirt fill eventually replaced the spectacular structure. BELOW: Early-day travelers wait at the Noyo River Tavern Station as a train approaches to take them to Fort Bragg. (Both: CWR)

Plummer, a partnership which owned substantial stands of redwoods. Thriving, Union proceeded to buy more tracts of timber and soon supplied much of America's redwood.

As the Union Lumber Company grew, so did Fort Bragg. Its residents voted to incorporate as a city in 1898 and Charles R. Johnson became its first mayor.

As crews downed the trees, the tracks followed logging operations inland along the natural route provided by Pudding Creek and then the Noyo River. The railroad began scheduling trips which were the great grandparents of today's Skunk tours. Singing and laughing, loggers and their girlfriends or families and other townspeople joined Sunday train outings over the short route into the redwoods.

The stands of trees suitable for logging became farther away from Fort Bragg, but the steep mountains blocked the extension of railroad tracks. Deciding to break the barrier with a tunnel, railroad officials called for workmen. Few local men, however, wanted to perform this dangerous and tedious work. Chinese workmen — famous for carving the Central Pacific tunnels through the High Sierra — were then called in for the construction.

They completed the 1,122-foot tunnel from Pudding Creek to the Noyo River in 1893. Designated Tunnel No. 1, it permitted the laying of tracks reaching deeper in the forest to extend and follow logging operations. The tracks happily provided longer excursion trips for Fort Bragg residents, who loved the redwoods and the railroad. By 1898, the line reached the Little North Fork of the Noyo River, 10 miles from Fort Bragg.

Life in the redwoods at this time was primitive when compared with more settled areas which boasted the comfort and luxury of rail service. Fort Bragg passengers bound to San Francisco or eastern centers travelled on the railroad to its end. There they transferred to a buckboard or stagecoach, which took them to Willits. From there they made a connection for another stagecoach which took them to Ukiah. Here they could board coaches of the Northwestern Pacific Railroad, which was being built northward from the San Francisco Bay area. The route not only was somewhat of an ordeal because of rough roads and the slow pace, but there were other hazards. Newspapers frequently reported that bandits stopped the stagecoaches and robbed passengers before

BELOW: An artist made this sketch of Fort Ross shortly after it was built, mostly of redwood, by the Russians. (California Historical Society)

EDWARD F. FREITAS
Photographer of the Redwoods

Many of the photographs in this book as well as in other publications about the California Western "Skunk" Railroad were taken by Edward F. Freitas, who spent most of his adult life working for the CWR and the Union Lumber Company and its successors, Boise Cascade Corporation and Georgia-Pacific Corporation. He passed away on February 14, 1991.

A native of Fort Bragg, Ed Freitas was graduated in 1942 from Fort Bragg High School and subsequently attended Santa Rosa Junior College and Montana State College. After World War II service in the U.S. Army, he was employed by the Union Lumber Company. There he worked as an equipment operator and from 1948 until its termination in 1972 was editor of *The Noyo Chief*, the company's magazine.

Mr. Freitas then worked as a fireman and motorman on the California Western, eventually becoming a locomotive engineer. He retired in 1986 due to illness, but his photography was not forsaken because it was his favorite hobby.

Mr. Freitas' photographs were widely used with numerous stories regarding Fort Bragg and the CWR.

Services were held at Our Lady of Good Counsel Catholic Church in Fort Bragg. Burial was in Rose Memorial Park, Fort Bragg. The casket bearers were Don Lopus, Maurice Fraga, Kenneth Winkler, Robert Reid, Gerald Allen, Charles Spencer, and Jerry Copeland.

He was survived by his wife, Angelina Freitas, and two sons, Robert Freitas of Fort Bragg and Steven Freitas of San Rafael.

Mr. Freitas' sparkling photographs of the California Western and of the redwoods will be eternal memorials of his creative life.

ABOVE: This early logging photograph shows how oxen pulled logs to mills from the forests. Railroads soon replaced the animals. (Bancroft Library) BELOW: A logger apparently brought his family to see a steam-operated cross-cutter. Large hand-powered saws once did this chore. (CWR)

Oxen pulled redwood logs down an incline in this view of early activities near Fort Bragg. These primitive methods soon yielded to locomotives. (Bancroft Library)

escaping into the depths of the forests.

The stage trip was an ordeal financially as well as physically. The stagecoach fair was $8.50 between Fort Bragg and Ukiah, which constituted less than a third of the total mileage to San Francisco. The rail fare from Ukiah to the Golden Gate bore a much more reasonable price tag — just $4.50. While that tariff may be a bargain by standards of the 1990s, it was expensive for the early 1900s. At that time $2.50

a day (not an hour) was a liveable wage, although loggers received more. The train was also a much more comfortable ride. Fort Bragg residents hoped that the California Western would soon reach Willits, where it would connect to the Northwestern Pacific when it reached that city. The rugged mountain country made railroad construction expensive and time-consuming. The Northwestern Pacific eventually would reach Eureka, but the original plan

ABOVE: A Northwestern Pacific train, typical of those which once operated from Sausalito to Eureka, heads through the redwood country when service was reaching a peak in the 1920s. The CWR was completed to connect with the NWP at Willits. (Southern Pacific Historical Collection) RIGHT: Here is a map of the NWP system.

to push the line up to Pacific Coast through Oregon would be abandoned because of excessive costs.

This was an era of growth and expansion, much of it fueled by the technology of the railroad. The Iron Horse made travel and freight-hauling much faster and cheaper than tedious treks with horse or mule power. Railroads were a generally popular preoccupation and subject of conversation with the American public in the early 1900s, just as apparatus for travel into space would capture imaginations a century later. Spectacular displays of large and ornate trains kindled a fascination over trains that burned for years. Crack passenger trains were going into service throughout the nation; new speculation

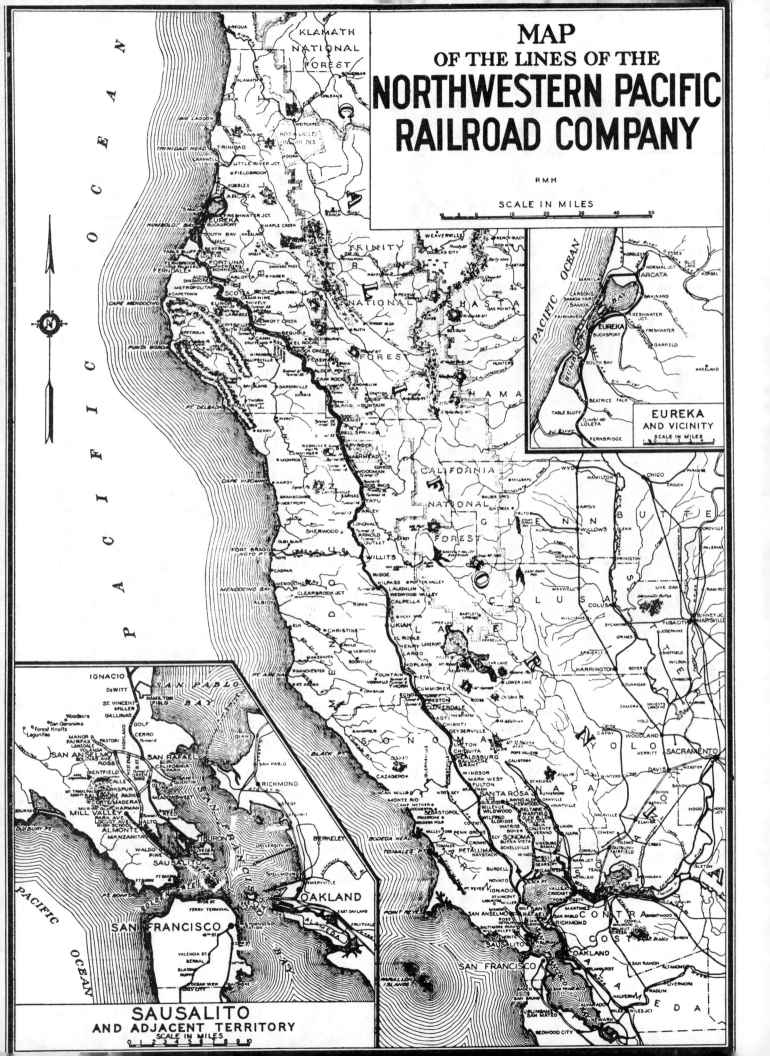

MAP
OF THE LINES OF THE
NORTHWESTERN PACIFIC
RAILROAD COMPANY

RMH

SCALE IN MILES

EUREKA
AND VICINITY

SAUSALITO
AND ADJACENT TERRITORY

Charles R. Johnson introduced improved logging methods, helped found Fort Bragg, and started the California Western Railroad.

developed daily over proposed lines.

The presence of a railroad signaled growth for a community that would be doomed without one. The Iron Horse opened new vistas in isolated towns, carrying residents quickly and relatively safely to the romanticized metropolitan centers. Much of a community's activities centered around the railroad depot, where townspeople traditionally gathered during idle hours to survey newcomers arriving on the train.

Residents of every city rated a railroad as a status symbol, and the people of Fort Bragg were no exception.

Fort Bragg residents yearned for rail connections to San Francisco, the shopping, business, and cultural center of the Pacific Coast. They visualized not only the pleasant trip from Fort Bragg in a comfortable railroad coach, but they were also convinced that thousands from the Bay area would come north either for sightseeing or to settle permanently for life in the forests.

Residents gratefully noted and saluted each new mile of track which made their homes closer to connections with San Francisco, even though some had doubts regarding the curving and difficult route up the canyon of the Noyo River.

"Locomotive No. 1 has made several trips up Cannon Ball Gulch lately," the Fort Bragg Advocate reported after an 1899 extension. "Mrs. Fred Severance is the first lady to ride over this piece of road. She had good nerve."

Besides watching the progress of the Fort Bragg Railroad, citizens also eyed news of a projected rail line that would connect San Francisco with Eureka and, eventually, Seattle. Two competing rail lines were on the drawing boards. E.J. Harriman, president of the Southern Pacific, planned one and E.P. Ripley, head of the Santa Fe, planned the other. As expensive as it might be to the big companies paying the bills, the competition was quite welcome to residents of the redwood country who wanted rails for passengers and freight. Perhaps the tremendous costs of building and maintaining the railroad from Fort Bragg frightened the Southern Pacific and Santa Fe over the price tags of pushing rival lines through similar terrain to reach Eureka. The two giants in 1906 reached a compromise that opened the way for the eagerly-awaited rail route. Under the agreement, the lines formed the jointly-owned Northwestern Pacific to build and operate the link. This brought great heart to loggers and other residents.

The Union Lumber Company recognized the value of a rail connection to the NWP and thence to all America for Fort Bragg residents and for shipping redwood products. As part of the efforts to complete

Locomotive 22 wears a screen on its smoke stack to arrest the chance of fires when it operated in the forests. BELOW: Despite their relative novelty in the early twentieth century, cameras appeared frequently in the woods. These construction workers stopped for a photograph by a pile of ties. (Both Photographs: CWR)

ABOVE: Mack Rail Bus M-80, which became famous as the Skunk, rolls over a bridge soon after going into service in 1926. It was then initially olive green. RIGHT: This photograph of M-80 was made soon after it went into operation. Note the hood that was distinctive of Mack Trucks in the era. (Both: CWR)

Here is a 1904 photograph of the 512-ton S.S. Brunswick, which flew the flag of the Union Lumber Company's National Steamship line from 1903 until 1931.

a rail link to Willits, on June 5, 1905, officers incorporated the California-Western Railroad and Navigation Company. This firm assumed operation of the Fort Bragg Railroad. Despite the "navigation" in its name, the new company never operated ships, even though Union Lumber did so until 1940 through its National Steamship subsidiary. In 1948, the firm dropped the hyphen and reference to navigation and became simply the California Western Railroad.

Before the railroad was built, ships indeed

provided an important means of transporting both people and products between Fort Bragg and the outside world — the latter being epitomized by San Francisco.

Before establishing the CWR, the Union Lumber Company looked to the sea by its 1901 incorporation of the National Steamship Company, a firm that during approximately forty years of operation owned eight ships. The sea offered a relatively easy means of travel during the late nineteenth century when there were few motorized vehicles, highways were yet to be invented, and rails still were to be stretched from Fort Bragg to civilization.

Travelers much preferred comfortable quarters aboard a ship, even though the sea often was rough, to a rougher stagecoach trip over rutted roads and the prospects of bandits, and primitive inns between Fort Bragg and the Bay of San Francisco. It was also easier to load lumber on a ship than to divide it among several mule-drawn wagons that would creep over the primitive roads.

First ship to join the fleet was the 512-ton Brunswick, built at North Bend, Oregon, in 1898 and purchased five years later by Union's National subsidiary. The company acquired the National City, a 310-ton vessel built in 1888 at San Francisco, in 1906 — just in time to help when the earthquake jolted Fort Bragg. In 1908 the company acquired the 415-ton Coquille River, constructed in 1896, and the Arctic, built in 1901. Three ships christened Noyo flew the National flag at varying times. A gas schooner, Coquet, was the company's eighth ship.

Travel and shipping on the vessels was hardly what one expects today on an ocean voyage. The seas pound the waters of northern California, and the coast abounds with rocks against which stormy waves can smash ships. In addition, there are treacherous currents which can sweep ships toward rocks or the rugged shores. There are numerous records of tragedies involving wrecks on the northern California coast involving ships in the nineteenth and early twentieth centuries. The first Noyo, Fort Bragg newspapers reported in late January 1896, hit a storm 36 hours after leaving the city with several passengers and a redwood cargo on its deck. Waves washed away part of the cargo and flooded the engine room. Despite the ordeal, the passengers and ship reached port safely.

The first Noyo was wrecked in 1914, and the second Noyo, a 1,419 steam schooner purchased in 1923, was wrecked in 1935. The Arctic was wrecked

A California Western locomotive steams past an area where construction was under way. Note how the trees had been logged, thanks to the convenience of the railroad. (CWR)

Passengers enjoy one of the many excursion trips between Fort Bragg and Willits which were offered when the line was completed. (CWR)

on the rocks in 1922. The Union Lumber Company gradually moved out of the maritime industry. The Hammond Lumber Company purchased the Brunswick in 1931, and Peru acquired the National City in 1918. The third Noyo was the last ship to fly the company's flag. A 1,484-ton vessel purchased in 1935, it was sold five years later to Thailand.

The Iron Horse — and the Skunk — rather than ships reigned supreme in the redwoods.

Hardly was the California Western organized than it was called to duty during the 1906 earthquake that severely damaged San Francisco and also rocked the Mendocino coast. A fire threatened the Fort Bragg lumber mills, but a locomotive fortunately was under steam at the time of the quake. It sped to the scene and pumped water on the flames before damage could spread.

Pushing the tracks to Willits proved a difficult and expensive task. Each mile brought new challenges of rough terrain, rivers, and streams to cross. The tracks

This historic photograph was taken December 19, 1911, as Locomotive No. 5 sped from Fort Bragg to Willits with the first passengers to travel the new Redwood Route. (California Western Railroad)

in 1910 reached Burbeck, just five air line miles from the proposed terminus in Willits. Construction engineers announced that so steep were the mountains that it would take 12 miles of tracks to travel that five miles and reach the city. Nevertheless, CWR officials decided to complete the line. The railroad conquered the final mountain barrier early in 1910 with the 795-foot long Tunnel No. 2, with local laborers constructing the project.

Building the California Western was indeed a costly task in regard to labor, financing, and engineering skills. While the transcontinental railroads received government subsidies and generally followed easier terrain, the CWR received its entire financing from its owner, the Union Lumber Company. Logging along the way, of course, helped pay the costs. Redwood lumber, preferred over pine for railway ties because of its durability, came, of course, from the Union mills. The mountainous terrain was the CWR's greatest enemy during construction. Longer railroads ordinarily had extensive flat areas to cover, a fact that helped absorb the higher costs of pushing tracks through mountainous or other rough terrain. Since the entire route offered virtually no flat areas, the construction price tag was high. It took 40 miles of track to reach a destination only 22 airline miles away. There were countless curves as the tracks, hugging the natural route of the Noyo River canyon, stretched farther into the mountains. The tracks crossed back and forth over the river to take advantage of the most favorable terrain. Many thirty-three and thirty-four degree curves — unusually sharp for a railroad — carried the tracks through the forests and up the mountains. One trestle curved in a perfect letter "S" to help conquer the mountain route. This trestle eventually was replaced with a land fill.

The cost of building the California Western added up to an expensive project — probably much more costly than the records show. The CWR was capitalized at $1 million, which would have valued the railroad and its equipment at $40,000 a mile, or substantially less than the $100,000 per mile average capitalization for railroads at the time. A 1914 California Railroad Commission report reflected the CWR's high value. The company estimated the cost for replacing the entire railroad would be $1,876,860. The state agency, which often halved valuations placed by other railroads, very nearly agreed. The commission estimated that the price tag for reproducing the CWR tracks and equipment would be $1,724,900. This, of course, was in 1914 dollars. The cost would be many times that amount in dollars of the 1990s.

Regardless of costs, the CWR pushed onward, and in late 1911 finally reached Willits.

Completion of the railroad had been the prime subject of talk for months in Fort Bragg business circles, lodges, women's club meetings, and in the

The crowd at Willits gave an enthusiastic welcome to the first train from Fort Bragg in 1911, gathering around the depot when this picture was made. (CWR)

Stretching through the great redwood forests, the CWR tracks brought new vistas when they were completed in 1911. LEFT: A train filled with merry-makers rolls over an immense trestle on the CWR line. Note the short cars required in order to negotiate the sharp curves. (Both Photographs: CWR)

It was a pleasant summer day in the 1950s when this photograph was taken as Skunk M-100 rolled past a backdrop of redwooods and other trees.

The Redwood Route has changed little with the years. This is an early day picture of the station at Grove.

ILLUSTRATED

CALIFORNIA WESTERN RAILROAD & NAVIGATION Cº

THRO THE REDWOODS

CAMPING HUNTING FISHING

logging camps. Everyone in Fort Bragg wanted to be among the first to ride behind the Iron Horse on its historic initial trip from the Pacific Ocean at Fort Bragg, through the redwoods and over the mountains to Willits. Even by installing benches on the three flat cars to supplement the seats on the two passenger coaches, there would be room for only 150 lucky guests.

For years, the matter of having a railroad had occupied the minds and daily conversations of almost everyone in Fort Bragg and Willits. The early years of the twentieth century were ones when there were few automobiles and people travelling any distance had the choice of going by horse and buggy or train, if they were able to reach the rails. In the case of Fort Bragg, those rails were forty miles away in Willits.

Few people mentioned the word "automobile." The Ford Motor Company, whose Model T would revolutionize personal transportation, would not be formed until 1903.

Since Fort Bragg had a harbor, it had the advantage of allowing frequent trips down the coast to San Francisco. Residents, of course, preferred the ocean voyage over the one by buggy over poorly graded roads with sharp, body-shaking curves around mountains. The April 18, 1894, edition of the Fort Bragg Advocate described one such trip being sponsored by the Independent Order of Odd Fellows, one of the town's social organizations. The newspaper explained that the steamer Daisy Kimball would leave Fort Bragg Saturday at 4:30 a.m, arriving an hour later at Mendocino and 7:30 a.m. at Point Arena so that more passengers could board the vessel. The ship would arrive in San Francisco at 6 o'clock in the evening on the same day.

LEFT: The cover of this 1917 CWR brochure suggested the many attractions awaiting rail travelers to the redwoods. RIGHT: The Redwood Route.

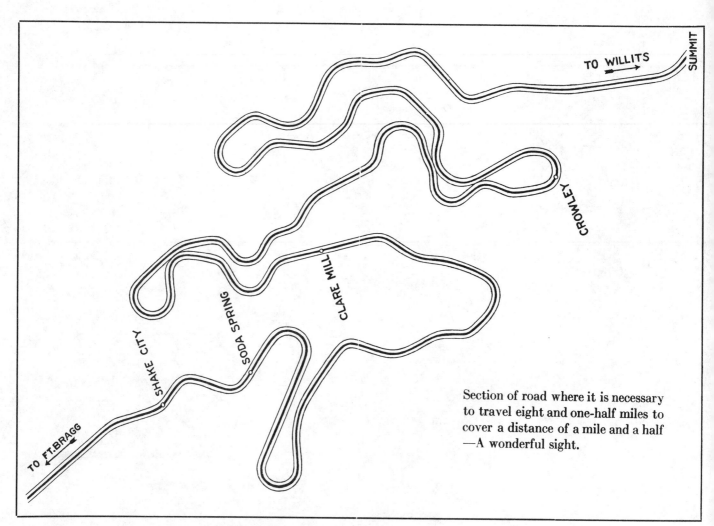

Section of road where it is necessary to travel eight and one-half miles to cover a distance of a mile and a half —A wonderful sight.

STATIONS, DISTANCES, ELEVATION, Etc.

DISTANCE	STATIONS	ELEVATION
.0	Fort Bragg	80
f 1.0	Pudding Creek	20
f 3.4	Glen Blair Jct.	27
f 6.7	South Fork	39
f 9.0	Ranch	64
f 10.0	Redwood Lodge	78
f 12.6	Grove	125
f 15.0	Camp Three	199
f 16.0	Camp Four	228
f 18.0	Alpine	264
f 20.0	Camp Seven	292
f 20.5	Noyo Lodge	308
21.2	Northspur	322
f 21.3	Noyo River Tavern	330
23.9	Irmulco	408
f 26.7	Shake City	560
f 27.7	Burbeck	688
f 28.7	Soda Springs	808
f 30.2	Clare Mill	1023
f 32.6	Crowley	1375
f 33.8	Crater	1513
f 35.2	Summit	1740
f 37.5	Rodgers	1433
40.0	Willits	1364

DISTANCE	STATIONS		ELEVATION
.0	Willits	N.W.P.	1364
25.55	Ukiah	"	610
54.31	Cloverdale	"	315
71.51	Healdsburg	"	99
85.76	Santa Rosa	"	151
137.87	San Francisco	"	4

DISTANCE	STATIONS	ELEVATION
.0	Fort Bragg	80
1.0	Pudding Creek	20
3.4	Glen Blair Jct.	27
6.5	Glen Blair	130

f—Train stops only on signal or to leave passengers.
Passenger train service in either direction daily.
Connects with the Northwestern Pacific Railroad at Willits.
Stage connections are made at Fort Bragg for points up and down the coast.

California Western Railroad and Navigation Company

FORT BRAGG, CALIFORNIA

1011 CROCKER BLDG., SAN FRANCISCO, CAL., PHONE SUTTER 6170
Issued 1917

Adding to the fun aboard the ship was the Mendocino Brass Band, a popular group in a time when various groups were formed for community entertainment. In the newspaper's same issue, an article described a play presented by the drama club of another Fort Bragg social group, the Improved Order of Red Men.

Incidentally, the Red Men's Hall in Fort Bragg was a pride of the city. Completed in 1894, the building included a 30 by 40-foot stage, beneath which were dressing rooms. Its members boasted that the theater facilities were the best of its type north of San Francisco.

The cost for the Odd Fellows' round trip jaunt to San Francisco was $4, but before describing the fare as a bargain, look at wages for the time. They ranged from $8 to $12 for a six-day week That's correct, the pay was for a week, not an hour or a day, and there were no medical benefits!

Even that pay was much better than it had been ten or fifteen years earlier. In the early 1880s, the weekly pay for a logger was approximately $7.50 a week (again, not per day) for a twelve-hour, six-day week. The pay included meals and lodging. Extending this pay to an annual basis is difficult because there was no guaranteed wage and work often was interrupted by rains or shutdowns caused by lack of demand for timber.

The average teacher in some respects fared a bit better than the loggers in that he or she worked for the school year. A teacher's pay was about $10 a week, but that, of course, did not include room and board.

The 1800s and early 1900s, by the way, were tough on the average person as compared to the

A 1917 folder issued by the CWR showed the wonders of The Redwood Route. LEFT: This section gave prospective travelers an idea of the twisting route and listed mileages and elevations. RIGHT: This illustration showed an excursion train stopping so that passenegers could look down on the curving track.

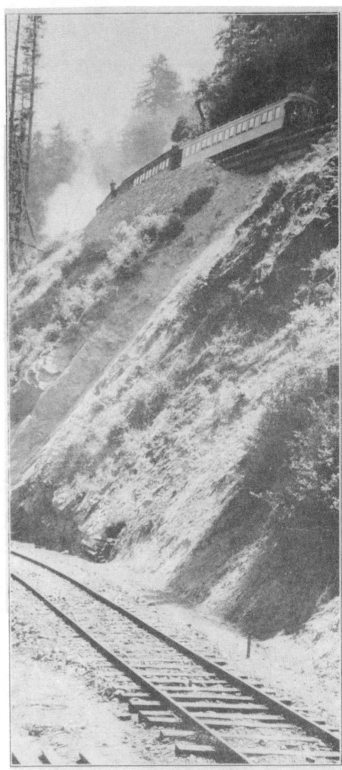

Where one track is almost directly over the track lower down.

16

45

This is one of the water tanks built along The Redwood Route for locomotives. BELOW: This 1962 photograph show how waters of the Noyo River can rage after heavy rainfall. (Both Photographs by Craig A. Robinson)

46

To show the immense size of a downed giant, this party of early twentieth century travellers went, horses and all, on top of the tree.

decades ahead. The editor of the Advocate noted that a state prison guard assaulted by an inmate lost his right arm and the legislature passed a measure awarding him $10,000 as compensation. Governor Markham, however, vetoed the legislation because he regarded the amount as excessive.

By the 1920s loggers earned $150 to $200 a month, out of which they paid approximately $1 daily for board and room. The rate of pay dipped during the Great Depression years of the 1930s, then climbed with the building boom that fol-

lowed World War II.

In recent years, quotas imposed by environmentalists and others on the volume of logging and timber supplies has resulted in spasmodic layoffs.

Besides speculation as to when a railroad from Fort Bragg would connect to other parts of America, articles in the Advocate often discussed ways to improve the city. One frequent subject was the danger of pot holes on streets and the need for more gravel on them. The newspaper

Locomotive 22, acquired by the California Western in 1921 and scrapped in 1950, wears a protective cap to guard against fires while operating. (California Western Railroad)

also emphasized the need for sidewalks. One such article said, "What a shame it is, in a wooded country like this, to have the school children wading back and forth from school in mud, in many places ankle deep. We need a good walk up Laurel Street and Redwood Avenue to the school house." The reference to the "wooded country" was to laying wooden sidewalks, the usual technique at the time. The newspaper went so far as to suggest that the city adopt laws requiring property owners to build sidewalks to help improve Fort Bragg in 1896, the paper advised readers of a study that warned that smoking cigarettes was injurious to one's health. The article suggested that young men who felt a need to use tobacco should use cigars or pipes.

Another news story recounted how a brave dog named Hank rescued his pal, a cat called Tom, by carrying him by the neck to safety from a fire.

While people in other parts of California were aware of the beauty of the redwoods a century and more ago, relatively few visitors made it to Fort Bragg. The overland trip was a rugged one

The Union Lumber Company made these houses available to employees and their families for the bargain rental of $2.50 a month during the early twentieth century.

48

These happy travellers boarded flat cars converted for passenger use so they could join a standing-room-only excursion into the redwoods after the CWR was completed. (California Western)

over primitive roads, and the ocean voyage required passage over rough seas where it was not uncommon for ships to be dashed against rocks. And there was no railroad, of course, that could bring the visitors.

The citizens of Fort Bragg showed much interest in civic life. One 1894 newspaper article pointed out that there were six candidates seeking election as town marshal, and another six running for city trustees. As in other cities at the time, there were numerous lodges and social groups in

which people were involved. Fort Bragg, then as now, was a happy city where people relished the many things it offered. When scanning pages of the Fort Bragg Advocate-News of today, one is impressed in the obituaries section to read of people who were born in the Mendocino Coast area and spent their entire lives there.

As explained above, practically every person in town wanted to be on the first train to Willits when the line was completed in 1911. The task of selecting the chosen few from the city's 2,400 residents was assigned to Fred C. White, at the time superintendent of the Union Lumber Company and president of the California Western Railroad from 1917 to 1927. Those fortunate enough to be invited for the trip rode free as guests of the CWR and its then parent, the Union Lumber Company. Considerable status went to the person who could boast that he or she went aboard for the historic trip.

Passenger service was inaugurated December 19, 1911, with J. C. French, CWR superintendent, directing the operation. The crew included John Pimental, who left his native Azores for America as a youth. Falling in love with the redwoods, he was so eager to remain in Fort Bragg that he took a job laying tracks for the California Western. His enthusiasm was rewarded, and after just nine days he was offered a position as a CWR trainmen. The others in the crew were Fred Hanson, the conductor, who joined the railroad in 1905 after working on other logging lines; he enjoyed the redwoods so much he didn't seek another job. Ed

Locomotive 12 took two coaches carrying rail fans on the Ten Mile line north of Fort Bragg in 1949, the year it was abandoned. (Bill Pennington Collection)

The time was May 1947, and a California Western train of logging cars was heading south to Fort Bragg over the Pudding Creek Bridge by the ocean. (Bill Pennington Collection) BELOW: Here is the way the same scene looked in the early 1990s. (Photograph by the Author)

Here is the California Western depot in Fort Bragg in the early 1960s before the Skunk insignia replaced the long-time CWR logo. (Photograph by the Author)

This 1949 photograph was made during a rail fan trip to the Union Lumber Company's Ten Mile Camp the year the line was abandoned. (Bill Pennington Collection)

Hendrickson was engineer for the first run.

The honor of pulling the first coaches over the line went to Engine No. 5, a 90,000-pound Schenectady Locomotive Company product built in 1880 and which the CWR acquired in 1906.

At 9:15 a.m. Fred Hanson called "All Aboard," even though the cars were filled and there was no room for more passengers.

The locomotive's bell rang happily; its horn gave a deep blast. The passengers cheered, and so did the waving bystanders left behind to make the trip another day. The train rolled out of the depot,

its ringing bell almost drowned out by the cheering passengers and spectators.

While Ed Henrickson sat in the cab as the official engineer, J.C. French, the CWR superintendent, took the throttle for the happy and historic trip.

The train chugged along the familiar and everbeautiful route by Pudding Creek, through Tunnel No. 1, and then alongside the curves of the Noyo River. It passed Alpine, Irmulco, and Burbank. Then it began to move through territory that was unfamiliar to the passengers. Ahead was the

53

Skunk M-80, the first rail bus purchased by the California Western, had just left Tunnel No. 1 when this photograph was taken in the late 1940s. (Bill Pennington Collection) RIGHT: Artist Richard Datin in 1963 produced this pen-and-ink rendition of the same scene.

Skunk M-80, damaged beyond repair in a 1964 collision, was unloading passengers when this picture was taken in the 1950s. (Redwood Empire Association)

recently-completed Tunnel 2.

The passengers cheered.

The train crew members smiled.

Once through the tunnel, the train began to descend towards Willits.

Reflecting the sentiments of its readers, the Advocate reported the occasion of the first trip to Willits with the headline, "A Great Day of Rejoicing."

"It was a day looked forward to for years by the old residents of Fort Bragg with eager anticipation," the editor wrote, "and when it did finally come, it brought with it all the pleasures and happiness of years stored up in realization of such an

An early 1900s photograph was made of this train with cars loaded with freshly-cut trees. BELOW: Trucks as well as railroads haul trees to a mill. Downed trees were piled four high on this truck's trailer.

Skunk M-100, built in 1925, awaits passengers during the 1950s at the CWR depot in Fort Bragg. (James Gayner Collection) RIGHT: Here are engineering drawings for the rail bus. BELOW: Loggers in this early 1900s scene combined horse power and steam power.

A locomotive pulls a train of box cars, timber, and passenger coaches over The Redwood Route in this photograph that was probably made during the 1950s.

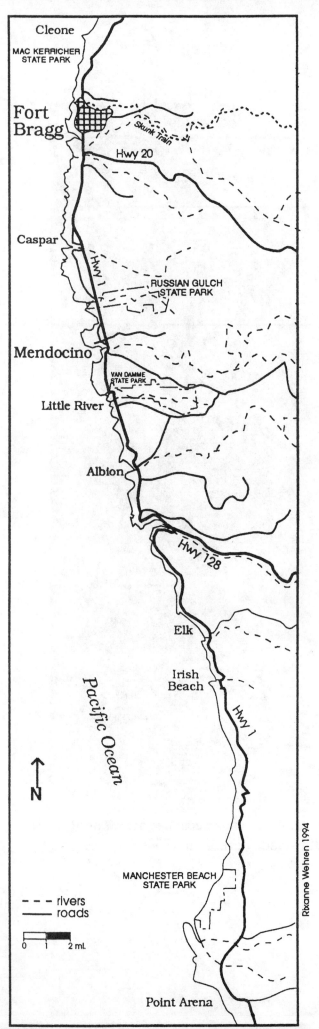

Cleone

MAC KERRICHER STATE PARK

Fort Bragg

Skunk Train

Hwy 20

Caspar

Hwy 1

RUSSIAN GULCH STATE PARK

Mendocino

VAN DAMME STATE PARK

Little River

Albion

Hwy 128

Elk

Irish Beach

Hwy 1

Pacific Ocean

↑
N

Rixanne Wehren 1994

MANCHESTER BEACH STATE PARK

- - - rivers
——— roads

0 1 2 ml.

Point Arena

important event.

"It was a great day in the broadest sense of the word," continued the editor, warming up to the subject, "and those in that party, we venture, will always refer to it as one of the happiest days of their lives, when the coast of Mendocino County, was bound with steel rails, on one of the greatest and most scenic routes in the State of California, with the interior, giving direct communications with the outside world."

The Advocate's editor described the trip with detail and enthusiasm.

"There is loop after loop on the road before reaching the summit," he reported. The construction presented some very difficult engineering problems...This part of the world is simply grand from a scenic point of view, and will be the tourists delight after the road is opened next spring for travel..."

The editor wrote no truer words as he described the scenery, for the line was to delight travelers' for many decades to come.

The locomotive's whistle echoed over the countryside, alerting nearly everyone. An eager crowd waited at Willits, and the town's community band began to play as the Iron Horse from the shores of the Pacific chugged into town.

The passengers were so thrilled that they hardly noticed that the lack of ballast on new sections of the track made the last part of the trip a bit rough.

"Old men acted in playful moods like boys," reported the Advocate, "and the whole population was enthusiastic in the demonstration made."

The Iron Horse from the Pacific had arrived.

Highlighting the celebration was a lunch at the Hotel Willits attended by C.R. Johnson and his daughter, Emily.

For the return to Fort Bragg, Mr. French again

This map shows the places that are in easy driving distance of Fort Bragg. (Collection of Sharon Brewer, publisher of the Fort Bragg Advocate-News; used with permission)

took the throttle of the locomotive, handling it, the Advocate reported, "very carefully over the road and proving himself to be a master mechanic in his line.

That afternoon the railroad played host for a banquet at Fort Bragg's Hotel Windsor. Still rollicking, townspeople celebrated the great occasion with a dance in Red Men's Hall.

One person missing from the celebration, however, was the CWR's superintendent, J.C. French. While outwardly calm during the trek, he was concerned over his passengers' safety on sections of the unballasted track. He excused himself from the festivities in order to recover from a headache.

There were few railroads at the time, particularly in the rugged mountains along the Mendocino Coast where roads were few and poor. The completion of the railroad heralded a new era of easier travel for passengers and more accessible markets for the region's timber.

Despite the success of the initial trip and the Advocate's editor's prediction that service would start in the spring, Fort Bragg had to wait for more fun on its new steel highway. The winter proved to be a wet one. Heavy rains not only delayed the ballasting, but also brought landslides.

The railroad was regarded as safe enough for regular traffic only by mid-summer of 1912, a full six months after its unofficial opening.

The first through trip open to the general public was headed for a Fourth of July celebration at Willits.

"This is a great chance to take a ride over the new road," reported the Fort Bragg Advocate, "running through the great redwoods and spend a day with our neighbors."

The train left Fort Bragg at 7 a.m., arriving in Willits at 9:30 a.m. for a day marked with basket

Skunk Rail Car M-100 rolls through the redwoods in this 1950s photograph. (Watson and Meehan Collection)

61

Skunk M-100 rolls out of Tunnel No. 1 during the 1950s.

Locomotive 45 heads into Willits after the trip through the redwoods from Fort Bragg. (Photograph by the Author) When steam reigned on the California Western, this locomotive hauled logs on the railroad's Ten Mile River branch. (James Gayner Collection)

The Mendocino County Museum, on Commercial Avenue east of the CWR depot, preserves and displays artifacts of the redwood country. BELOW: These steam engines and other objects were used in the early logging days. (Both Photographs by the Author) RIGHT: Here is a collection of passes issued to CWR employees. In return, the CWR issued courtesy passes to employees of other railroads.

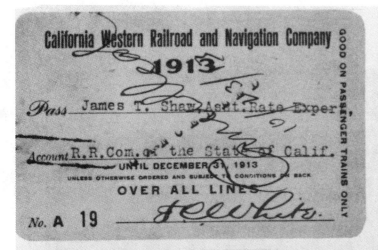

California Western Railroad and Navigation Company

1913

GOOD ON PASSENGER TRAINS ONLY

Pass James T. Shaw, Asst. Rate Exper.

Account R.R. Com. of the State of Calif.

UNTIL DECEMBER 31, 1913
UNLESS OTHERWISE ORDERED AND SUBJECT TO CONDITIONS ON BACK

OVER ALL LINES

No. A 19

OVER ALL LINES

F. C. White

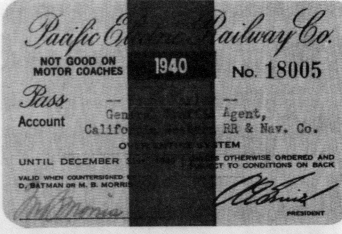

Pacific Electric Railway Co.

NOT GOOD ON MOTOR COACHES

1940

No. 18005

Pass ——————

Account Gen——— Agent,
Califo——— RR & Nav. Co.

OVER ———— SYSTEM

UNTIL DECEMBER 3— UNLESS OTHERWISE ORDERED AND SUBJECT TO CONDITIONS ON BACK

VALID WHEN COUNTERSIGNED
D. BATMAN OR M. B. MORRIS

PRESIDENT

NORTHWESTERN PACIFIC
RAILROAD COMPANY

REDWOOD EMPIRE ROUTE

1940-1941   X 870

PASS   ---Mr. H. H. Sanborn---

ACCOUNT   President, C.W.RR.& N. Co.

BETWEEN ALL STATIONS UNTIL DECEMBER 31, 1941, UNLESS OTHERWISE LIMITED BELOW
AND SUBJECT TO CONDITIONS ON BACK.

VALID WHEN COUNTERSIGNED BY
T. F. EAGEN
COUNTERSIGNED

PRESIDENT & GENERAL MANAGER

Southern Pacific Lines
IN

1940-1941 TEXAS AND LOUISIANA   GOX 3938

Pass   Mr. H. H. Sanborn. - - -
President.
California Western R.R. & Nav. Co.

EXPIRES DECEMBER 31ST, 1941. UNLESS OTHERWISE LIMITED

EXECUTIVE VICE PRESIDENT

THE DENVER AND RIO GRANDE WESTERN RAILROAD COMPANY
WILSON McCARTHY AND HENRY SWAN, TRUSTEES

1941-42   B 2660

THIS PASS ACCEPTED BY ME FOR USE SUBJECT TO CONDITIONS ON BACK

PASS H. H. Sanborn,
President
California Western RR. & Nav. Co.

UNTIL DECEMBER 31, 1942, UNLESS OTHERWISE ORDERED OR SPECIFIED
HEREON AND SUBJECT TO CONDITIONS ON BACK

VALID WHEN COUNTERSIGNED BY
J. M. HADDEN OR E. E. EMERSON
COUNTERSIGNED

Wilson McCarthy
TRUSTEE

CALIFORNIA WESTERN RAILROAD
AND NAVIGATION CO.

CALIFORNIA THE REDWOOD WESTERN

1941-1942   NO. 3

PASS Mr. H. H. Sanborn,
President,
Calif. West. R. R. & N. Co.

UNTIL DECEMBER 31, 1942
UNLESS OTHERWISE ORDERED
SUBJECT TO CONDITIONS ON BACK

GENERAL MANAGER

UNION PACIFIC RAILROAD

NOT GOOD ON
"STREAMLINERS" OR "FORTY-NINER"

1941   AX 2113

PASS Mrs. H. H. Sanborn****
Wife of President
California Western R.R.& Nav. Co.

OVER ALL LINES UNTIL JANUARY 31, 1942 UNLESS OTHERWISE
ORDERED OR SPECIFIED HEREON

ADDRESS San Francisco REQUEST OF hhs d-31

VALID WHEN COUNTERSIGNED BY F. J. ROACH OR B. L. HERBERT

COUNTERSIGNATURE

PRESIDENT

YOSEMITE VALLEY

1937-1938   RAILWAY COMPANY   302

PASS   Mr. W. S. Taylor
General Traffic Agent
California Western RR & Navigation Co.

ADDRESS Fort Bragg

UNTIL DECEMBER 31, 1938
UNLESS OTHERWISE ORDERED
SUBJECT TO CONDITIONS ON BACK

VICE PRESIDENT AND GENERAL MANAGER

Skunk Rail Bus M-80 speeds along the CWR route against a background of redwood trees in this 1950s photograph. (Redwood Empire Association) RIGHT: This section of a U.S. Geological Service topographic map shows the CWR tracks heading inland from Fort Bragg.

lunches, fireworks, sports events, and the inevitable patriotic speeches. The return trip departed from Willits at 6 a.m.

A special inducement to acquaint the public with the line provided round-trip tickets for $3, the usual cost of traveling just one way. The CWR announced that those wishing to stay more than a day and return by rails would be charged $4.50, a bargain rate when compared to the fees

for riding the less-thrilling and rougher-riding stagecoaches.

A week later, on July 10, a reverse version of the excursion was offered. A special train ran from Willits to introduce residents to the charms of seaside Fort Bragg. The completed railroad helped people of the two cities to get acquainted, and it also brought new commerce to Fort Bragg. On July 17 the first passenger train with a freight

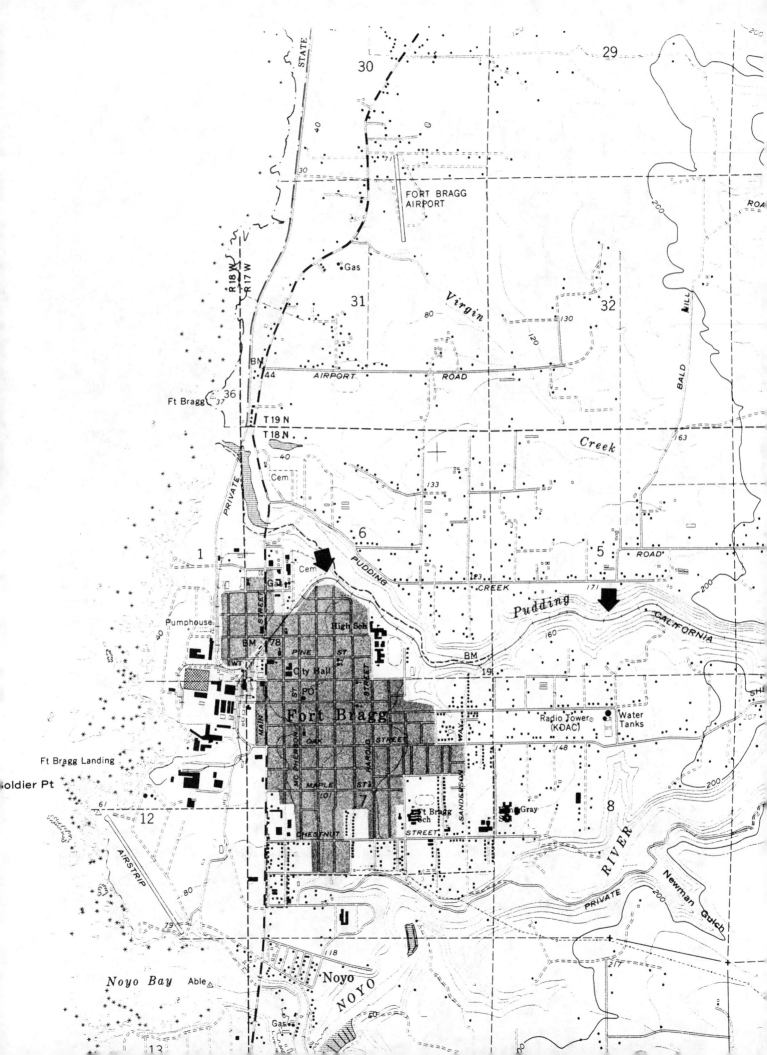

A train rolls alongside the Pacific Ocean en route to Fort Bragg on the CWR's Ten Mile River branch shortly before the line was abandoned in 1949. (James Gayner Collection) RIGHT: A portion of the Noyo Hill Quadrangle of a U.S. Geological Survey topographic map shows the California Western tracks hugging the Noyo River. At the top of the map, note Glen Blair, once the center of logging activities and an area served by rails. BELOW: Pulled by a diesel locomotive, this train was crossing a street in Fort Bragg after the trip through the redwoods. (Photograph by the Author)

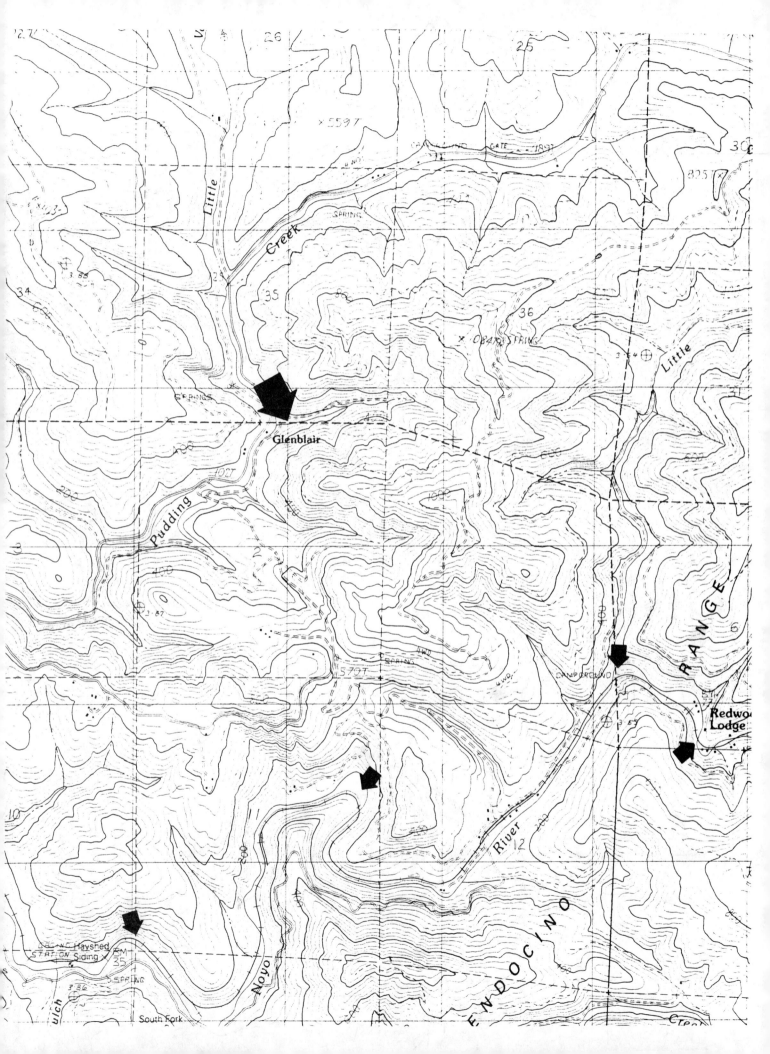

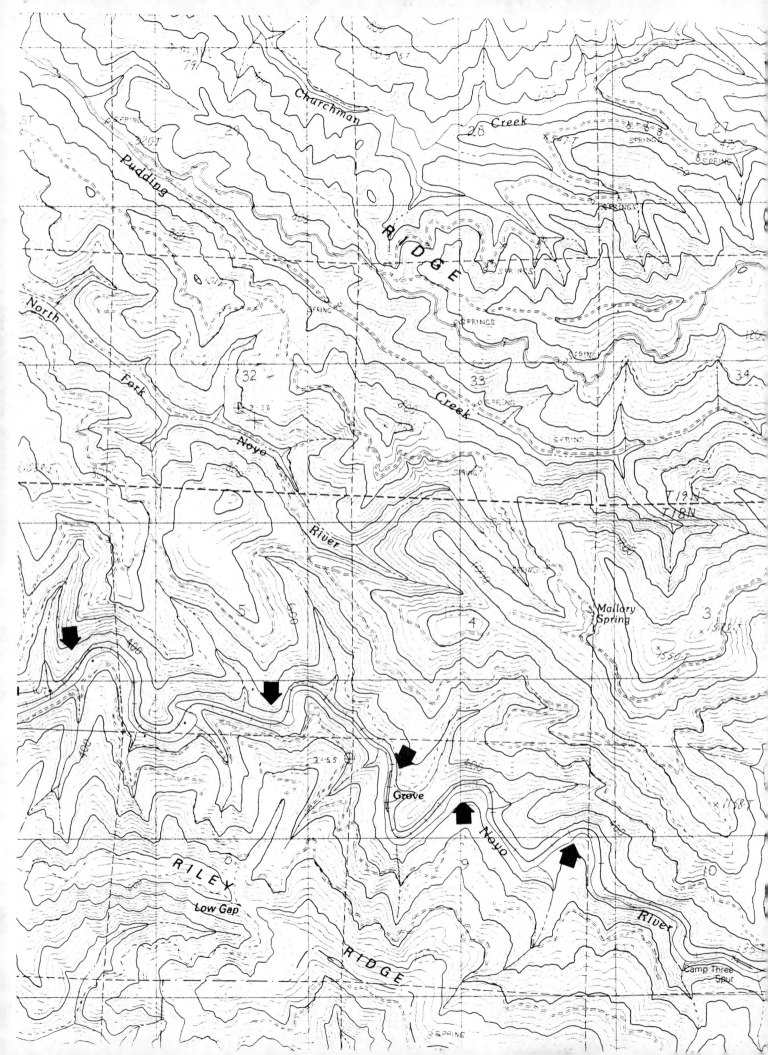

Locomotive No. 22 goes over the Pudding Creek Bridge in 1949 as it makes the final trip on the CWR's Ten Mile River branch, carrying logging equipment for use elsewhere. (James Gayner Collection) LEFT: This is an eastern portion of the Noyo Hill Quadrangle of a U.S. Geological Survey topographic map. Note the stations and the track winding with the Noyo River.

car attached rolled over the route. The cargo was 82 barrels of wine bound from Cloverdale to Fort Bragg.

John Pimental and Fred Hanson in a 1963 interview with the author recalled the excitement of that first day and told how the passengers were as thrilled as kids would be on their first ride at Disneyland. The two veteran railroaders also told of their pleasure working for the California Western and enjoying operating equipment in the redwoods through the years.

All concerned, townspeople, loggers, railroaders, and assorted out of town visitors, hailed the line as a success, not only for linking Fort Bragg and Willits with a steel highway but also for enabling people to take delight in taking excursions through the redwood country. Jaunts through the magnificent big trees were as popular then as they are now. The railroad attracted many sight-seers from the San Francisco Bay area and beyond.

In 1913, the Northwestern Pacific Railroad

the California Western: Fort Bragg to Willits

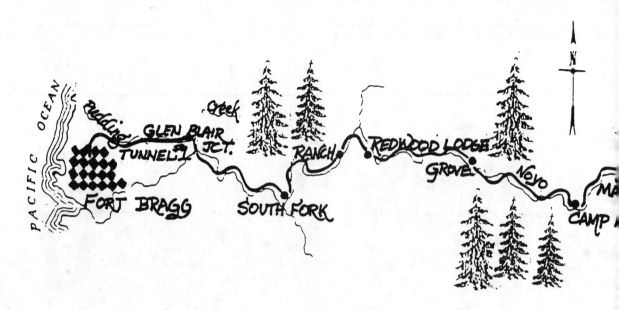

```
MILES:-Fort Bragg/Willits--STATION----------------ELEVATION
          0....40.0.....Fort Bragg...................80
          1.0....39.0.....Pudding Creek................20
          3.4....36.6.....Glen Blair Junction.........27
          6.6....33.4.....South Fork...................39
          9.0....31.0.....Ranch........................64
         10.0....30.0.....Redwood Lodge................78
         12.7....27.3.....Grove.......................125
         15.0....25.0.....Camp Three..................199
         16.0....24.0.....Camp Four...................228
         16.4....23.6.....Camp Noyo...................229
         18.1....21.9.....Alpine......................264
         20.0....20.0.....Camp Seven..................292
         20.5....19.5.....Noyo Lodge..................308
         21.3....18.7.....Northspur...................322
         23.9....16.1.....Irmulco.....................408
         26.8....13.2.....Shake City..................560
         27.7....12.3.....Burbeck.....................688
         28.7....11.3.....Soda Springs................808
         30.4.....9.6.....Clare Mill................1,023
         32.6.....7.4.....Crowley...................1,375
         33.8.....6.2.....Crater....................1,513
         35.4.....4.6.....Summit....................1,740
         37.5.....2.5.....Rodgers...................1,433
         40.0.......0.....Willits...................1,362
```

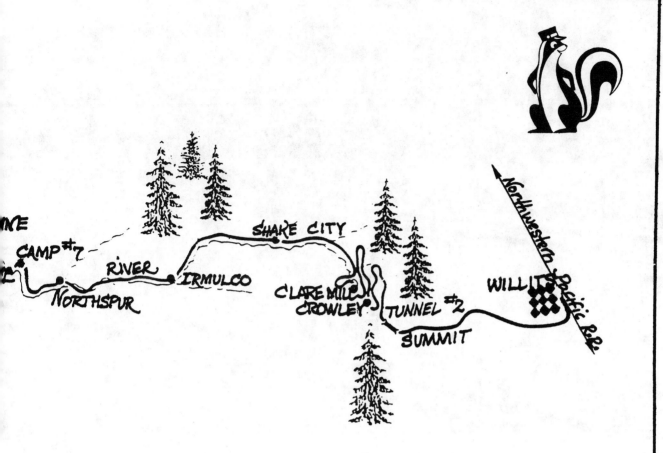

Mileage-to/from-Fort-Bragg/Willits-&-Other-Cities

Map by Victoria Crump-McCarthy

These CWR freight cars with wooden sides were photographed in 1923 shortly after being rebuilt. (California Western Collection) RIGHT: The eastern half of a portion of the Northspur Quadrangle of a U. S. Geological Typographical map shows the settlement of Northspur, which is half way between Fort Bragg and Willits. BELOW: The departure of Locomotive No. 3 proudly pulling coaches 42 and 43 became a familiar sight in the early twentieth century. (California Western Collection)

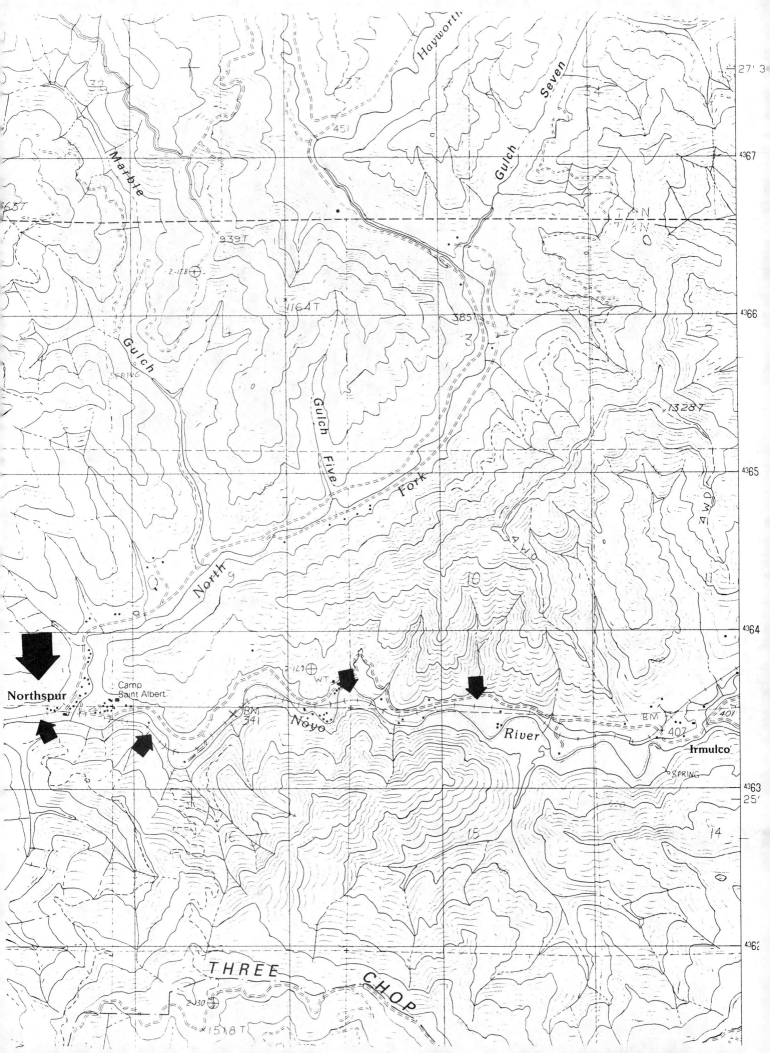

Skunk M-200 was at the Willits depot when this photograph was made in the 1950s. The locomotive is on the adjacent Northwestern Pacific tracks.

Crew members check for signals after passengers board The Super Skunk steam train.

from San Francisco was completed to Willits, at last providing direct access and cheaper service to the tracks throughout America, both for passengers and for timber products. Laborers continued building the NWP northward. The immense cost of construction through the rugged mountains, however, forced its owners to abandon the original goal of reaching Oregon and rail connections to northern sections of America. The NWP eventually was completed to Eureka at a point just north of Arcata.

When the CWR tracks at Willits met those of the Northwestern Pacific, it attracted more passengers than only the local ones. Arriving from San Francisco, people were enchanted, just as are visitors today, with the Fort Bragg redwood country.

By late July, the CWR attracted a crowd of 400

San Franciscans in a single day.

"The many excursionists were given full benefit of California's greatest scenery on the California Western Railroad and Navigation Company's open air observation cars," the Advocate reported, referring to the flat cars topped with improvised chairs, "and every moment of the ride through the virgin redwoods of the upper Noyo and along its winding way."

Even the residents of the redwood never tire of its charms.

"Each and every member of the party was loud in its praises of the scenic beauty of the new road," the newspaper noted proudly.

Virtually every railway in America drew new settlers to its area, for the presence of steel highways greatly increased the desirability of any region. The CWR's completion was no exception to the rule, and the line was seized upon as an ideal reason for settlers and investors to acquire property destined for development with the expected population boom.

The Union Lumber Company offered numerous parcels of cleared land for sale to be developed into residential, dairy, or orchard property. Real estate brokers eagerly took up the sales pitch.

J.L. Johnson, a real estate broker in San Francisco, placed this ad in the Advocate:

"Fort Bragg is growing fast and has all the facilities that can be found in any modern town...18 miles from Willits, the California Western Railroad and Navigation Company has sub-divided 2,000 acres of cut overland with the idea of attracting the best class of settlers, and every facility will be offered by the railway company to see that any one who purchases this land is aided in getting properly, comfortably, and profitably settled."

As the years passed, more and more out-of-state visitors learned the glory of the redwoods. Travel-wise passengers on the Northwestern

A high-climber starts up a redwood tree to start work during an early twentieth century logging operation. (University of California School of Forestry)

Pacific made stopovers in Willits so they could ride the famed CWR route through the forests amid the spectacular mountains.

Appropriately, the California Western's official

Skunk M-80, having had its olive green paint replaced by bright yellow, awaits passengers at the Willits depot during the 1960s.

slogan became "The Redwood Route." The slogan helped distinguish the red and black circular insignia emblazoned on the CWR's freight cars and stationery.

Its status as a common carrier also earned the California Western the right of exchanging passes with other railroads, ranging from short lines to transcontinental railways.

The era's pass privilege enabled the employees of short lines throughout America to travel without charge on railroads throughout the nation. In exchange, those associated with the major railroads found themselves with passes valid for the dubious right to ride short lines, many in isolated regions devoid of attractions. The Redwood Route was different. Many transcontinental rail officials complained that exchanging passes was one-sided because of the difference in company

trackage and scope of operations. There were few complaints from railroaders who used passes on the California Western, for even though the line was just 40 miles long it traversed a portion of the world's most beautiful and spectacular scenery.

New creatures began making their way into the redwoods: Model T's and other low priced cars chugged and puffed over crude roads which became better by the year providing new alternatives for travel. Fewer people rode the railroads generally and many nights the beautiful Pullman coach left Fort Bragg for San Francisco with few berths occupied. While 38,822 passengers rode the CWR in 1923, the line carried only 20,097 people in 1925. Pullman service from Fort Bragg ended November 3, 1928. In view of the declining passenger service, CWR officials sought ways to reduce the expenses. One major expense covered maintaining the route for daily passenger service when rains and floods damaged the track. While railroads devoted exclusively to logging could delay moving freight cars, a line such as the CWR that carried passengers had to move quickly with repairs to restore service. Despite declining passenger service, the CWR had the expense of operating a locomotive and coach even though only a handful of passengers rode on each trip.

One suggestion for cutting expenses came from Mack Trucks, Inc., the producer of heavy trucks whose trademark was a sturdy bulldog.

Seeking new markets, Mack designed and in 1920 began building gasoline-powered buses mounted on rail wheels. These vehicles offered savings by substituting a driver for the engineer, fireman, and brakeman required for a conventional steam locomotive train. There would be further savings through the costs of maintaining only a bus instead of a locomotive and its coaches. In addition, the buses could start and stop easier, therefore being better suited for short line travel with numerous stops.

Other companies also began building similar rail buses, which were the predecessors of today's diesel-powered locomotives at a time when steam engines were virtually the only means of motive power.

Mack completed a 35-passenger rail bus, tagged "Model ACX" for its particular design, on October 19, 1923, at its plant in Allentown, Pennsylvania. Complete with toilet facilities and a baggage compartment, its price was $12,524. It was a good buy because it eliminated the need for coaches and supporting personnel.

Searching for ways to reduce expenses yet maintain passenger service, CWR general manager Carleton A. Curtis went east to inspect the bus. Favorably impressed, he arranged for a demonstration on The Redwood Route in 1925. The

The Mack rail bus, adorned with a circular "The Redwood Route" emblem, posed for this picture after entering CWR service in 1926. (CWR)

How to Reach the Depots

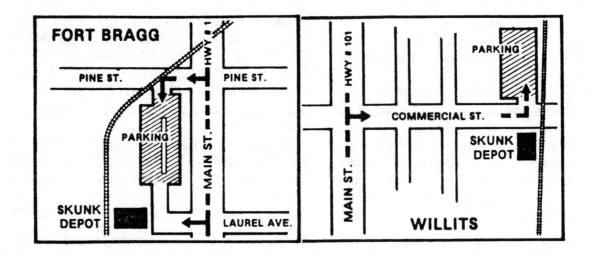

These maps show how visitors can reach the California Western depots in Fort Bragg and Willits.

line officially purchased the vehicle on December 30, 1925. Numbered "M-80," the letter indicating that it carried its own motive power, the bus entered service with passengers and onlookers both amused and pleased. Townspeople applied nicknames ranging from "Galloping Goose" to "Tin Lizzy" before finding one that not only seemed suitable but also helped to bring fame to the California Western.

The name, of course, was "The Skunk."

There is no documentation of how or with whom the name originated. The most popular story hold that trainmen who were familiar with steam locomotives said that the gas fumes were "like the odor of a skunk."

However the name started, The Skunk — originally garbed in olive green paint — faithfully began serving passengers. The blast of its horn became familiar and welcome along the Redwood Route.

While automobiles reduced the number of passengers on the California Western, so did the Great Depression of the 1930s and early 1940s. With less money, both visitors and Fort Bragg residents stayed at home rather than travel.

When other rail buses became available, the CWR purchased them for stand-by service. These were the acquisitions, all assigned "M" prefixes to note that they carried their own motive power.

M-100, was acquired in 1936 after having been constructed in 1926 by the Edwards Railway Motor Car Company of Sanford, North Carolina. The Morehead and North Fork Railroad of Kentucky

80

This Studebaker automobile was equipped with rail wheels so that it could operate on the Glen Blair Lumber Company trackage, which connected with the California Western tracks. In the car are members of the Blair family, touring their empire on a spring day in 1913. (Hugh Tolford Collection)

When it snows --

Winter can bring snow to the higher levels of The Redwood Route, and sometimes even to Willits. These photographs were made during the teens and twenties. ABOVE: Snow covered the ground at this stop for water. UPPER LEFT: A locomotive in the snow awaits coaches. LOWER LEFT: The train stopped for passengers to take this photograph. (CWR)

and snows!

This early 1960s photograph shows Skunk M-100 travelling on The Redwood Route. Note the track below (right center) that the train must travel to gain elevation. (Watson and Meehan Collection) BELOW: Ray Regalia was a CWR official for many years and helped develop the Super Skunk. (RIGHT) The Super Skunk, pictured soon after its 1965 inauguration, prepares to leave Fort Bragg. (CWR)

Skunks M-200 and M-80 meet at Northspur, approximately midway between Fort Bragg and Willits, in the late 1950s. (Bill Pennington Collection)

used it until its passenger volume decreased.

M-200, purchased in 1941, was built in 1927 by the Skagit Iron and Steel Works of Sedro-Wooley, Washington, for the Longview, Portland, and Northern Railroad of Oregon. The Trona Railroad in California's Mojave Desert used it until ending rail passenger service.

M-300, placed in service in 1963, was built in 1935 by the American Car and Foundry Company for the Aberdeen and Rockfish Railroad of North Carolina. The Salt Lake, Garfield, and Western Railroad's Saltair line to the Great Salt Lake later used it. Before going into CWR service, a diesel engine was installed to replace the original gasoline engine.

Despite the attractions of rails and redwoods, few people who resided away from the Mendocino Coast knew of the California Western until the 1950s when fame suddenly arrived. This celebrity status came through articles in Sunset Magazine, the National

Geographic, Trains, Model Railroader, and other publications. In addition, the CWR became better known through its use in the 1948 motion picture, Johnny Belinda, which won an Academy Award for Jane Wyman.

The California Western through the years has served as a popular location for several motion pictures. These films include the 1974 Walt Disney production Runaway on the Rogue River and the 1984 Paramount picture Racing with the Moon.

Passenger volume soared as fame arrived. In 1953, before the flow of articles on the Skunk, the CWR carried only 13,440 passengers. Eight years later it hauled 44,359 people — well above the 1923 peak mark — and was nudging the 50,000 mark.

Meanwhile, "progress" began to overtake motive power on the Redwood Route. The California Western purchased two diesel locomotives in 1949 and in 1956 acquired its third diesel. Coincidentally, it retired its last steam locomotives.

The Skunk rail buses reigned, carrying passengers between Fort Bragg and Willits. The diesel locomotives, at least for the time, served only freight trains.

As fame approached, the rail buses also began to sparkle visually. Their olive-green paint in the 1940s was replaced with yellow bodies and silver roofs. A final attractive touch for the buses came in 1959 with the addition of caricatures of a skunk wearing a conductor's hat.

The California Western in effect became Fort Bragg's second industry, the first being logging. While thousands of visitors came to ride the Skunks, more thousands came to photograph or merely look at them. Motels, restaurants, and other businesses opened to serve the travelers. Even model railroaders eyed the CWR. The Model Engineering Works of Monrovia, California, produced a HO scale model of Skunk M-80 with fascinating detail down to the Skunk insignia. Model Trains, published by Kalmbach Publishing Company in Waukesha, Wisconsin, in a September 1955 article by Andy Anderson suggested building a model layout based on the California Western. The layout featured the

Refreshments and souvenirs are available during the stopover at Northspur, approximately halfway between Fort Bragg and Willits. The facility has been operated for years by the Pratt family. Here are (from left) Diana Ballard-Doll, "Mama" Doll, and Leonora Pratt. RIGHT: The Super Skunk rolls through a meadow against a background of the forest. (Photograph by Larry Welborn)

line's two tunnels, water towers, and redwood structures.

The author noted that one thing associated with the CWR that couldn't be bought at a hobby shop was "the spirit of friendliness" associated with the line.

Despite the crowds that came to ride, profits eluded the California Western because the buses could not carry enough passengers to offset the tremendous cost of maintaining the right of way. Floods and landslides continually plagued the railroad. The situation became more difficult when Skunk M-80 was destroyed in a head-on crash with Skunk M-100 on September 26, 1964. The cause of the accident was one bus over-running a meeting point. The CWR promptly instituted precautions to protect riders from other accidents, but the fact remained that passenger capacity fell sharply with the loss of the unit. The wrecked M-80 remained in

the California Western yard at Fort Bragg until June 1966. Officials then decided the bus could not be rebuilt and junked it. Rebuilt, the M-100 returned to service. Coincidentally, Skunk M-200 left CWR service January 11, 1975, and was donated to the Pacific Locomotive Society for use at its Castro Point facility.

A solution to the lack of capacity to carry more passengers came in 1966 from Ray A. Regalia, a long-time CWR employee and at the time assistant general manager, and manager from 1974 to 1977. To accommodate more passengers and thereby generate more revenue, the CWR would bring back steam power and conventional passenger coaches.

Thus the Super Skunk came into being.

Finding a suitable steam locomotive was no easy task since their production stopped years ago. After a search, the CWR located a Mikado-type 2-8-2

ABOVE: Skunk M-200 made this stop for a photograph in the 1950s or early 1960s. (James Gayner Collection) BELOW: Here is the engineer's view from Skunk M-100. (Photograph by the Author.

The California Western in 1949 acquired diesel locomotives, which replaced steam for freight service. These two diesels were carrying finished lumber and freight car from Fort Bragg to Willits during the 1960s. (CWR)

super-heated Baldwin previously used by the Medford Corporation, an Oregon timber company. The oil burning locomotive, previously numbered "3," was rebuilt and designated No. 45 following the California Western's numbering system. Engine 44, also a Baldwin 2-8-2, had been scrapped in 1952.

Obtaining coaches also presented a problem; longer cars could not negotiate the sharp CWR curves. Officials eventually found four 72-foot coaches built for the Erie Railroad in 1926 by the Standard Steel Car Company and previously numbered 2300, 2332, 2343, and 2344. San Francisco industrial designer William Landor and Associates supervised their refurbishing. Brilliant vermillion, cool red, gold, and black help create a feeling of nineteenth century elegance. The numbers 651, 652, 653, and 654 went onto the coaches, along with names from the forest through which they would travel: Cleone, Navarro, Noyo, and Sherwood.

On July 10, 1965, Super Skunk service started on the Redwood Route between Fort Bragg and Willits.

As hoped, the train lured thousands of riders. Two more coaches were promptly added. They were the Westport (No. 655) and DeHaven (No. 656). More coaches, numbered 681, 682, and 684, went into service in 1977.

Super Skunk service usually operates from late May until shortly after Labor Day, a time that attracts the most passengers. Skunk rail buses take over during the slower seasons.

For economy reasons, diesel locomotives generally supply motive power for Super Skunk operations in recent years. The steam locomotive burns 500 gallons of oil per trip, but a diesel

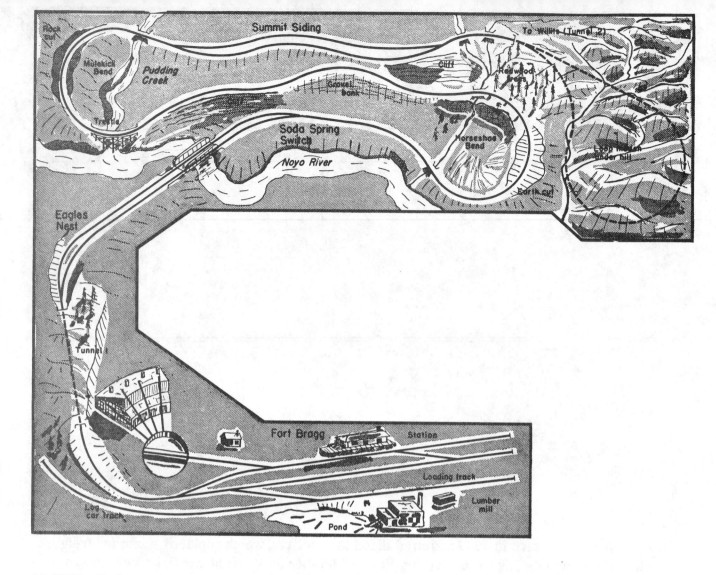

ABOVE: This suggested model train layout incorporates many CWR attraction, including Pudding Creek, the Noyo River, horseshoe bend turns, and mountains. (© Model Railroader Magazine; used by permission) BELOW: This HO scale model of Skunk M-80 was offered by the Model Engineering Works.

California Western Railroad crew members pose by diesel 57 after its purchase in 1974. Constructed by the Baldwin Locomotive Works in 1954, the engine previously was used by the Southern Pacific. It was reconditioned and repainted for CWR use. (CWR Photograph by Ed Freitas)

locomotive can cover the same distance by burning only 150 gallons. The difference in cost helps reduce the operating deficit. The CWR usually designates special days for offering steam service. Needless to say, steam service days are eagerly awaited and attract crowds.

As noted, the California Western has never been a big profit maker. The line earned $105,512 in 1912, a time before automobiles were in great use. It lost $20,466 in the depression year of 1938. Even with the return of prosperity after World War II, it alternately lost money and made profits.

The start of Super Skunk service appeared to signal the beginning of profitability. The ledger was on the plus side with approximately $59,000 and $90,000 in 1967 and 1969 respectively. But the Redwood Route also benefitted from freight traffic, notably the shipment of timber products. Trucks during the 1980s began carrying more and more products from the mills. As a result, the California Western reported losses ranging from $128,000 to $145,000 annually during the late 1980s.

Over the years, there were changes in the CWR management, the ownership of the redwood forests it served, and even in the railroad itself.

Charles R. Johnson, the man from Wisconsin who guided the development of the Union Lumber Company and the California Western, died of pneumonia February 1, 1940, just a few days before his 81st birthday. His son, Otis, born in 1885 at Fort Bragg, became president and served until his death in 1957. His son, C. Russell Johnson, then took over as president.

The late twentieth century was a time of acquisitions and mergers which would reach into the coastal redwood country. Boise-Cascade Corporation, a lumber conglomerate, acquired Union and the California Western in 1970, but sold them in 1973 to Georgia-Pacific Corporation, also a giant in the lumber industry.

In 1977, Georgia-Pacific leased the California Western to the Mendocino Coast Railway, saying it hoped the move would bring in management that could reduce losses and still permit passenger service to continue.

Serving as president of Mendocino Coast was

A stopover at **Northspur**, midway on the route, gives passengers time to snack before continuing or boarding a train to return to the departure point.

Even though conventional passenger trains returned to The Redwood Route, the faithful Skunks continued to operate. M-300 goes over a redwood-shaded bridge. (CWR Photograph by Ed Freitas)

Willis B. Kyle, whose holdings also consisted of short line railroads elsewhere in America. The staff included John D. Pacheco, auditor, and Henry Foltz, a veteran trainman, who was general manager from 1979 to 1989.

In June 1987 Georgia Pacific announced the sale of the California Western to the Kyle organization, which said the line would continue operating under the CWR name.

People of the Mendocino Coast cherished the California Western just they did the redwood forests, the fish-laden streams and rivers, and the churning waves of the Pacific which splashed against the rocky coast.

Perhaps some days they looked back at the happy days when the railroad was operated by the Johnson family-controlled Union Lumber Company and its local management was more a part of the

Generation after generation enjoys riding the California Western. ABOVE: The author's children, Victoria and John, look at CWR souvenirs after a ride during the early 1970s. BELOW: In the late 1990s, Victoria's son, Benjamin Lewis McCarthy, plays on a CWR caboose with the author's stepchildren, Andrew and Natalie Walker.

community. In those days the CWR did more than haul lumber and passengers. When a lumberjack was injured or a pregnant woman in a camp needed medical attention, a train was dispatched to take the patients to a hospital.

The era of community ownership returned in mid-1996 when a group of Fort Bragg and Willits people purchased the railroad from the Kyle interests.

Residents of both towns were overjoyed at the event!

The acquisition was led by Gary Milliman, city manager of Fort Bragg who resigned his office and became CWR president, and Sean Hogan, a Fort Bragg attorney and certified public accountant, who became the line's counsel. Lynn Hakin became chief operating officer.

Milliman was a former journalist whose father and grandfather had been involved in railroading. His wife, Carolyn, joined the CWR board of directors and also portrays "Twinkle the Skunk" in costume at the Fort Bragg depot and at community events.

A model railroader, Sean Hogan soon was able to run a railroad in more ways than one; he often worked as a brakeman. His wife, Janice M. Hogan, became corporate secretary and a member of the board of directors..

Lynn Hakin's grandfather, Allan C. Holmes, was a boiler maker with the California Western. She began her CWR career as a ticket clerk and train hostess, advancing through several positions.

Planning to take the CWR into the twenty-first century, the new owners purchased two additional passenger coaches.

The CWR also purchased two more diesel locomotives and signed a lease with the non-profit Roots of Motive Power to restore steam Locomotive 14. Gary Milliman also began negotiating to acquire two additional steam locomotives.

The Skunk railroad was getting better every day!

96

Engineer John Galliani and conductor King O. Nelson were checking rolling orders before Skunk M-100 departed the Fort Bragg depot on a 1963 trip. (Photograph by the Author)

When the time arrives to ride the Skunk, whether it is aboard a rail bus or behind a locomotive, you breathe deep at the expectation of taking the famous ride into the redwood forest.

You wisely made ticket reservations in advance, whether the trip would start in Fort Bragg or at the Willits end of the route.

At Fort Bragg a caricature of a saucy Skunk, appropriately wearing a conductor's cap, beams down approvingly from the roof of the depot.

Should you leave from Willits you'll park adjacent to the station on Commercial Street by the tracks which the California Western shares with the line which once carried passengers between San Francisco and Eureka. If you drive down Commercial Street you will find the Mendocino County Museum with displays relating to railroading and logging.

Before the trip, visitors in Fort Bragg or Willits will enjoy browsing through the shops. Many buildings were constructed of redwood grown in

nearby forests and follow architectural lines typical of the late nineteenth and early twentieth centuries.. Most stores are locally-owned, and are staffed by friendly sales people.

If you arrive from spring until early fall, the sparkling coaches of *The Super Skunk* await you or you may choose to ride in one of the picturesque rail buses.. Should you make the trip during other months, a rail bus will carry you..

Either way, your trip through the redwoods will hereafter be one of your fondest memories.

Wearing a bright red vest beneath the coat of his uniform, your conductor smiles happily as he collects tickets. He knows that this will be a memorable trip. The CWR policy is to sell only as many tickets as there are seats available, so you'll have no problem finding a seat.

As the train leaves the depot, its horn toots a warning signal to motorists. Passengers in the autos smile, and bystanders make photographs of

ABOVE: Starting in 1949, the CWR began to replace its steam locomotives with diesels. Built by the Baldwin Locomotive Works, these were the line's first diesels. BELOW: Skunk 200, pictured in the 1970, awaited passengers at Fort Bragg.

Bright and new, Skunk M-80 took time out to have this picture taken shortly after going into service in 1926. RIGHT: These are the engineering drawings for Skunk M-80. BELOW: Skunk M-80 heads up a steep, sharp curve soon after starting service. (Both Photographs: California Western)

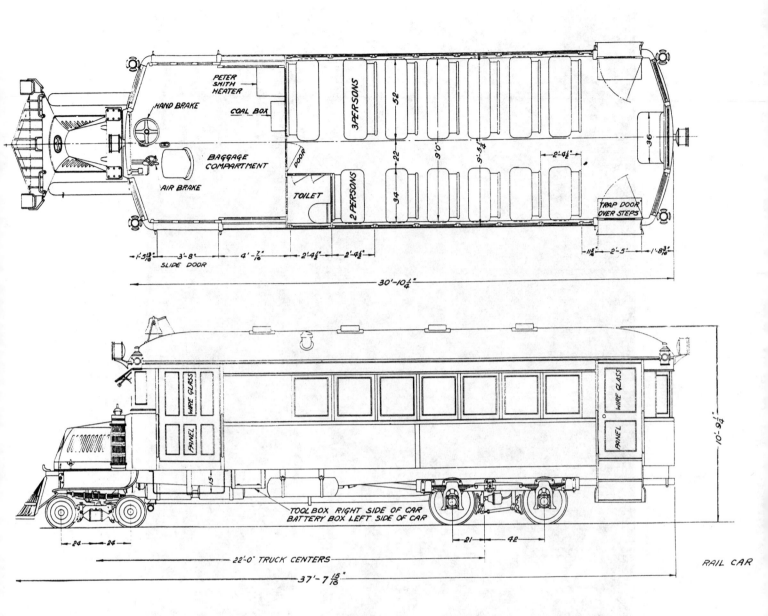

PETER
SMITH
HEATER

HAND BRAKE

COAL BOX

BAGGAGE
COMPARTMENT

AIR BRAKE

DOOR

TOILET

2 PERSONS

3 PERSONS

52

22

94

9'-0"

9'-5¾"

2'-4½"

36

TRAP DOOR
OVER STEPS

1'-5⅝"   3'-8"   4'-7⅞"   2'-4½"   2'-4½"   11¾"   2'-5"   1'-8¾"

SLIDE DOOR

30'-10¼"

PANEL WIRE GLASS

PANEL WIRE GLASS

10'-9¼"

15

TOOL BOX RIGHT SIDE OF CAR
BATTERY BOX LEFT SIDE OF CAR

24   24

21   42

22'-0" TRUCK CENTERS

RAIL CAR

37'-7 15/16"

The California Western Railroad was noted for its A-frame bridges, constructed without piles so that there would be no damage when heavy there were heavy rains. (Bill Pennington) RIGHT: A section of a U.S. Geological Survey Topographic map shows how the rail line curves and switches back to gain elevation as it nears Willits. Note the CWR stations along the line.

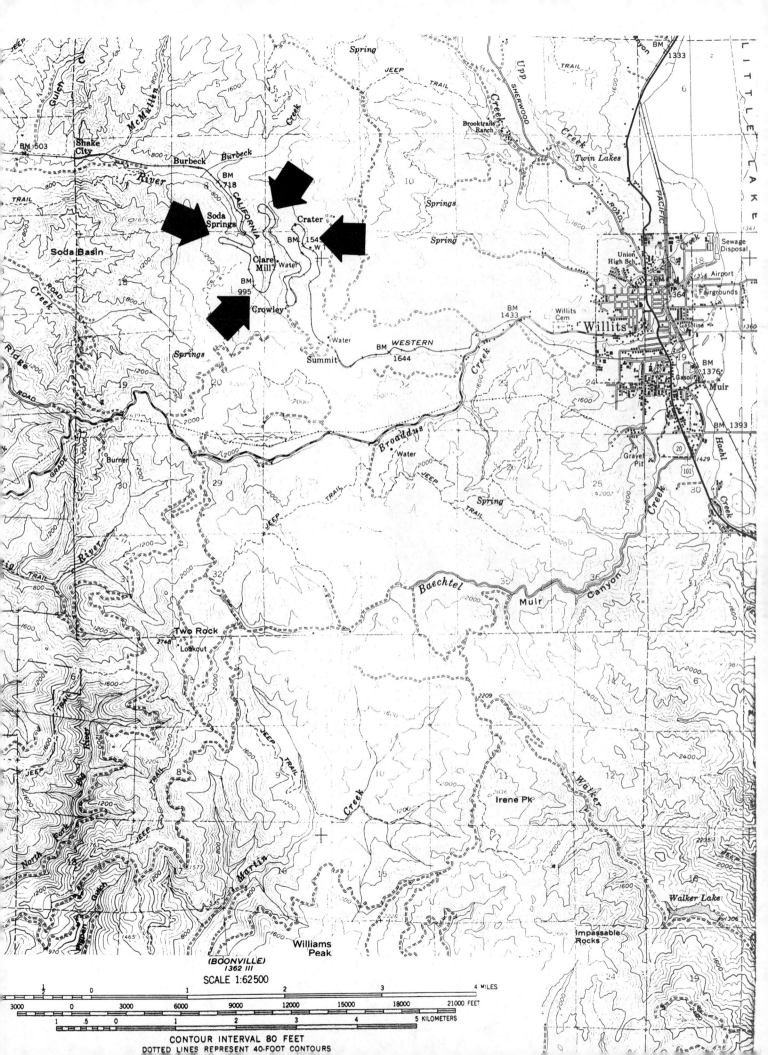

Gary Milliman, president of the California Western, discusses railroading with his wife, Carolyn, in her "Twinkle the Skunk" costume in which she greets passengers. She serves on the CWR board of directors.

the train crossing Highway 1. Many of the people are bound for the depot so that they can buy tickets for the trip on another day.

From the highway, the train skirts the northern section of Fort Bragg and chugs past the town's cemetery, where many loggers, trainmen, and their families are buried.

Alongside the train at Milepost 1 (Milepost 39 from Willits) is Pudding Creek. To the left, alongside the ocean, is a trestle used by the CWR's

Ten-Mile Branch until that rail line's abandonment in 1949. The train picks up speed, moving through forests of pine trees mixed with redwoods. A deserted roadbed departs from Milepost 3.4 (Milepost 36.6 from Willits); this is Glen Blair Junction, once the start of the rail line to the Glen Blair Lumber Company. This branch carried loggers four miles to the redwoods around Smith Creek.

Suddenly the passengers murmur; we have entered Tunnel No. 1, the 1,122-foot mountain-barrier breaker built by Chinese laborers at the beginning of the twentieth century.

Milepost 6.6 (33.4 miles from Willits) brings us to South Fork, near where the line terminated in the late nineteenth century and a favored place for Sunday outings by rail at the time.

The silence of the forest is broken only by the clickety-clack of the wheels on the tracks and the music of chirping birds. While The Redwood Route parallels the highway to Willits, it ranges from a mile or more from that asphalt artery. In effect, we are travelling in a world without automobiles. At times the redwoods give way to verdant green meadows; here a flock of sheep may be grazing, producing excellent wool in this higher, cooler elevation.

A child questions her mother, who replies that the squirrels are real and don't require batteries.

Ahead by the tracks we see a crouching cat, poised to pounce on a bird. The approaching train startles him, and the cat races through the waving grass for refuge beneath a cabin's foundation. You note to yourself that the cat's sure-fire knowledge of exactly where he can find safety means that the interruption of the train is almost a daily occurrence for him and one with which he has learned to live.

At Milepost 9.0 (Milepost 31.0 from Willits), the train reaches Ranch, at an elevation of 64 feet above sea level. The train passes Grove at Milepost 12.7 (from Willits, Milepost 27.3) at 125 feet

The Super Skunk train stops by the water tower at Northspur, midway between Fort Bragg and Willits. (CWR Photograph by Ed Frietas)

above sea level. Less than three miles further on, the train takes us 47 feet higher at Grove.

Most of these stations are marked with tiny open redwood stations built decades ago but still remarkably preserved. They are stations in name only since they have no attendants and only provide benches..

Along the way are cabins, whose residents reach them by train or primitive dirt roads. Here and there along the way the train skirts the Noyo River. Fishermen watch and wave as the train passes. These sportsmen catch salmon and steelhead during the open season in the summer.

When you ride the Super Skunk, you can walk through the coaches into what is probably the world's longest observation car: a complete rail car from which the top has been removed and on

which seats have been installed. From these cars you can glance upward through the great "tunnel" of redwoods trees stretching skyward.

Super Skunk passengers also hear a description of points of interest from hostesses who are virtual encyclopedias regarding the railroad and the redwoods

Camp Three (Milepost 15.0 from Fort Bragg, 25.0 miles from Willits) and Camp Four (Milepost 16.0 from Fort Bragg, 24.0 from Willits) represent logging points established as the line was pushed into the mountains from Fort Bragg. The train winds to climb 93 feet, covering four miles to reach Camp seven to Camp Four. The California Western's grades are steep, ranging up to 3.5 percent as compared to only 1 percent on most railroads. That's why the tracks wind around

105

An innovation in the late 1990s, "The Wedding Train" offers a railway passenger coach trip into the redwoods for the ceremony and reception. (Photograph by Leona Fern Walden, Mendocino, from the California Western Railroad)

slopes and curves for 40 miles to reach a destination just 27 air line miles away.

Here and there along the route you'll see the apple orchards planted soon after the CWR was completed. The cool climate produces tasty apples, and the railroad provided an excellent way to get them to market in an era when there were few roads and trucks were unreliable.

Milepost 16.4 (Milepost 23.6 from Willits) is Alpine, which at 264 feet above sea level means that the train has climbed 200 feet in only two miles, Here the railroad ended in the early days and

passengers boarded stagecoaches for the 22-mile trip to Willits and then south to San Francisco.

The train climbs; the air grows crisper and cooler. It rolls past Noyo Lodge at Milepost 20.5 (19.5 miles from Willits), and comes to Northspur at Milepost 21.3 (18.7 miles from Willits). The train that started from the other end of the line often arrives here at approximately the same time.

There is a "Y" track at this point where trains can change directions or pass. Incidentally, the CWR does not have a roundhouse. Instead, it uses the "Y"s and other track configurations to reverse the direction of equipment.

Northspur is a stop of approximately 45 minutes for passengers. Here the Pratt family established a refreshment facility where passengers can enjoy soft drinks, beer, and food, and shop for souvenirs. Riders then can continue to the end of the line or board another train to return to the station where they started,

This stop in the forest gives us an opportunity to meditate. The redwoods watch silently, as they have for centuries. If these big trees can think, they must be pleased that people have traveled to admire them in silent reverence.

The writer recalls a 1963 conversation with John Pimental, the likeable man who recalled how he left his home in the Azore Islands, fell in love with the redwoods, and stayed among them for the remainder of his life. He was the brakeman on the first through train when the line opened in 1911.

He could still remember the happy faces on the coaches on that first trip.

"They loved the redwoods," John Pimental smiled.

"I myself have never ceased marveling at the big trees despite more than sixty years among them," he continued, "and the people who come to ride our Skunk even these days say that our pictures fail to tell the story of their grandeur. One must see the redwoods to appreciate them."

What about the people who make the trek up

the Mendocino Coast during all the tomorrows?

"The redwoods will be here," John Pimental replied, still smiling, "and they will be bringing forth cries of joy, amazement, and pleasure a hundred years from now."

The train sounded its whistle. It was time to move on.

When the train rolls on, the right-of-way becomes steeper and steeper. You begin to realize what a battle it was to build the railway through this terrain.

Irmulco, at Milepost 23.9 (16.1 miles from Willits), was named for the Irvine and Muir Lumber Company which operated during the pioneer days. It is 408 feet above sea level, a climb of 100 feet in less than three miles. Leaving, the train rolls along one of the straightest stretches on the route – a one-mile run leading to Shake City at Milepost 26.8 from Fort Bragg (Milepost 13.2 from Willits). A mill here in the early logging days produced shakes for roofs and inspired the name. The route becomes steeper. Burbeck, at Milepost 27.7 (12.3 miles from Willits), is just a mile further but the elevation (688 feet above sea level) is 100 feet higher.

The passengers look up at the mountain side. Above is a stretch of track that the train will reach after only after eight miles of travel and twenty minutes of time. Soda Springs, at Milepost 28.7 (11.3 miles from Willits), brings the train to an elevation of 808 feet, a climb of 400 feet in just five miles. The train rolls on through Clare Mill at Milepost 32.6 (9.8 miles from Willits); Crowley at Milepost 32.6 (7.4 miles from Willits), and Crater at Milepost 33.8 (Milepost 6.2 from Willits)

Mile after mile of redwoods stretch out below, and you can understand why the trainmen on the California Western say they would never trade their jobs for others.

Milepost 35.4 (4.6 miles from Willits) brings the train to Summit, appropriately named because at 1,740 feet this is the top of The Redwood Route. During the peaks of winters, there often is snow in the area. Just ahead is Tunnel No. 2, carved in 1911 as the last barrier to completing the railroad. The tunnel is surfaced with cement.

The tracks begin to descend and at Milepost 37.5 (2.5 miles from Willits) go through Rodgers. The redwoods have given way to oaks and other trees, under which sheep graze tranquilly in the shade. In the spring the countryside appears to be ablaze with gold. Here are solid fields of California wild poppies, the state flower, stretching like an ocean of gold. The right-of-way nears the highway from Fort Bragg as it approaches Willits. As the train appears, motorists wave happily – probably wishing they had ridden the Skunk over The Redwood Route.

The train glides across Highway 101 and down the right-of-way to the depot at Willits. You alight at the Tyrolean – style station, constructed of clear-grain redwood lumber; it is as beautiful as the day when it was dedicated in 1916.

You've ridden The Redwood Route and seen the glory of the big trees, verdant meadows, grazing sheep and cattle, animals scurrying around shrubs, and the sparkling Noyo River – as only the Skunk can unveil them.

Your memories of The Redwood Route will be forever.

FOR MORE INFORMATION:

California Western Railroad
    For Train Reservations & Information
    Fort Bragg Depot: Willits Depot:
    Foot of Laurel St.   299 E. Commercial
    Fort Bragg 95437   Willits 95490
    (707) 964-6371   (707) 459-5248

Note: Phone numbers are subject to change. Verify numbers
with your telephone information operator.

Roster of California Western Motive Power

No.	Date Acquired	Type	Builder		Date Built	Cylinders
Steam Locomotives						
1	1905	0-4-0	Baldwin		1885	12x14
2 (1st)	1905	2-4-2	Baldwin		1887	12x20
2 (2nd)	1911	0-4-2	Baldwin		1901	17x24
3	1905	2-4-4	Baldwin		1884	14x20
4	1905	4-6-0	Hinkley		1883	16x24
5	1906	4-6-0	Schenectady		1880	18x24
6	1908	0-4-0	Mason		1868	14x22
7	1909	2-6-2	Baldwin		1909	15x22
8	1910	4-6-0	Southern Pacific		1869	18x24
9	1912	3-T Shay	Lima		1912	12x12
11	1913	2-6-2	Baldwin		1913	15x22
12	1914	2-6-2	Baldwin		1914	15x22
14	1938	2-6-2	Baldwin		1924	15x24
17: A renumbering of No. 7 in 1924						
21	1920	2-6-2	Baldwin		1920	18x24
22	1921	2-6-2	Baldwin		1921	18x24
23	1923	2-6-2	Baldwin		1923	18x24
36	1918	4-6-0	Baldwin		1890 (?)	19x24
38: A renumbering of No. 8 in 1924						
41 (1st)	1922	0-6-0	Baldwin		1901	16x24
41 (2nd)	1940	2-8-0	Baldwin		1920	18x22
44	1944	2-8-2	Baldwin		1930	19x24
45	1964	2-8-2	Baldwin		1964	19x24
46	1968	2-6-6-2 Mallet	Baldwin		1937	18x18x24
Diesel Locomotives				**Model**		
51	1949	0-4-0	Baldwin	S-7	1949	
52)	1949	2-4-2	Baldwin	S-7	1949	
53)	1956	0-4-2	Baldwin	S-10	1949	
54	1969	2-4-4	Baldwin	S-12	1969	
55	1970	4-6-0	Baldwin	RS-12	1955	
56	1970	4-6-0	Baldwin	RS-12	1955	
57	1970	0-4-0	Baldwin	S-12	1955	
61	1979	2-6-2	Alco	RS-11	1959	
62	1979	4-6-0	Alco	RS-11	1959	
63	1979	3-T Shay	Alco	RS-25	1959	
64	1989	2-6-2	EMD	GP-9	1955	
65	1990	2-6-2	EMD	GP-9	1955	
Rail Buses						
M-80	1925	0-4-0	Mack		1925	
M-100	1934	2-4-2	Edwards		1926	
M-200	1941	0-4-2	Skagit		1927	
M-300	1963	2-4-4	American Car & Foundry		1935	

Roster of California Western Motive Power

No.	Drivers	Tractive Effort	Weight	Boiler Pressure	Builder No.
Steam Locomotives					
1	42	7,500	50,000	130	7831
2 (1st)	42	7,560	60,000	130	8852
2 (2nd)	50	18,000	92,700	160	18618
3	42	n/a	70,000	n/a	n/a
4	57	n/a	115,000	n/a	n/a
5	57	20,000	163,000	170	2042
6	48	8,000	48,000	100	25
7	44	16,000	98,000	170	33390
8	57	20,000	117,000	165	2002
9	32	25,750	120,000	200	2547
11	44	16,000	98,000	170	39551
14	44	18,000	108,000	180	58050
17: A renumbering of No. 7 in 1924					
21	44	30,000	140,000	200	53277
22	44	30,000	140,000	200	54878
23	44	30,000	140,000	200	57553
36	44	22,000	135,000	160	9298
38: A renumbering of No. 8 in 1924					
41 (1st)	50	15,000	72,000	160	18760
41 (2nd)	42	26,000	121,000	180	53205
44	44	32,000	158,700	190	61306
45	48	30,000	150,000	200	58045
46	44	30,000	246,000	200	62064

No.	Tractive Effort	Weight	Horsepower	Builder No.
Diesel Locomotives				
51	50,000	200,000	750	74408
52)	50,000	200,000	750	74409
53)	58,750	235,000	1,000	74193
54	50,000	240,000	1,200	75823
55	57,500	240,000	1,200	76024
56	57,500	240,000	1,200	76105
57	57,500	240,000	1,200	n/a
61	57,500	260,000	1,800	n/a
62	57,500	260,000	1,800	n/a
63	57,500y	260,000	1,800	n/a
64	57,500	250,000	1,750	n/a
65	57,500	250,000	1,750	n/a

No.	Tractive Effort	Weight
Rail Buses		
M-80	29,000	See Notes
M-100	39,000	See Notes
M-200	41,590	See Notes
M-300	52,060	See Notes

(Continued on Next Page)

Notes to the Roster

Unlisted numbers in this roster are ones which were not assigned to motive power of the California Western Railroad.

Locomotives 1 and the 2 (1st) were wood burners eventually converted to using oil. The other steam locomotives were oil burners.

The Skunk rail buses originally were Pullman (olive) green. They were repainted yellow with silver roofs in the early 1940s.

No. 1: Known as the Sequoia when used by the Fort Bragg Railroad (the CWR's predecessor), this locomotive was sold in 1906 to Standish & Hickey, a lumber firm.

No. 2 (1st): The CWR acquired this locomotive from the Fort Bragg Railroad and sold it in 1910 to Irvine Muir Lumber Co.

No. 2 (2nd): Purchased in approximately 1911 from the California State Belt Railroad, the locomotive was scrapped in 1920.

No. 3: This locomotive was purchased in 1895 by the Fort Bragg Railroad, the CWR's predecessor, which sold it in 1918 to the Mendocino Lumber Co.

No. 4: The CWR acquired this locomotive in 1904 from the Southern Pacific and scrapped it in 1914.

No. 5: The locomotive was purchased in 1906 from the Southern Pacific of Arizona and scrapped in 1923.

No. 6: Purchased in 1908 from the Santa Fe Railroad, this locomotive was sold in 1910.

No. 7: This locomotive was acquired in 1909 and renumbered "17" in 1924.

No. 8: Previously used by the Central Pacific and Southern Pacific, this locomotive was acquired in 1910 and renumbered "38" in 1924. It was scrapped in 1942.

No. 9: Scrapped in 1917.

No. 11: Scrapped in 1947.

No. 12: Scrapped in 1950..

No. 14: Built in 1924, this locomotive was purchased in 1938 from the Fruit Growers Supply Co. The CWR sold it in 1956.

No. 17: Numbered "7" until 1924, the locomotive was scrapped in 1938.

No. 21: This locomotive was sold to Pan-American Engineering Co. in 1950.

No. 22: Scrapped in 1952.

No. 23. Scrapped in 1950.

No. 36: This locomotive was purchased in 1918 from the Colorado Midland Railroad, and sold in 1929 to the Little River Redwood Co.

No. 38: Numbered "8" until 1924, this locomotive was scrapped in 1942.

No. 41 (1st): Purchased in 1922 after being used on the Arizona and New Mexico and El Paso &

Southwestern railroads, this locomotive was scrapped in 1937.

No. 41 (2nd): This locomotive was purchased in 1940 from the Sierra Railroad and scrapped in 1950.

No. 44: This locomotive, previously used by the Lamm Lumber Co. of Modoc, Oregon, was acquired in 1944 and scrapped in 1952.

No. 45: Built for the Brownlee-Olds Lumber Co. of Medford, Oregon, this locomotive was acquired in 1964 from the firm's successor, Medford Corporation. It was rebuilt for Super Skunk service.

No. 46: This locomotive was constructed for the Weyerhouser Timber Co. and later used by Rayonier, Inc., at its operations at Hoquiam, Washington. The CWR purchased it from Rayonier in 1968 for Super Skunk service. In 1986 it was donated to the Pacific Southwest Railway Museum in San Diego.

No. 51.: This locomotive was scrapped after being damaged in a January 1970 accident which also involved Locomotives 52 and 54.

No. 52: This locomotive also was scrapped after being damaged in an accident involving Locomotives 51 and 54 in January 1970.

No. 53: Once used by the United States government, this locomotive was acquired in 1956 through Pan-American Engineering Co. The CWR sold it in 1985 to John Bradley of Willits.

No. 54: This locomotive, built for the Wabash Railroad, was scrapped after being damaged in the 1970 accident that also involved Locomotives 51 and 52.

No. 55: This locomotive was built for the McCloud River Railroad.

No. 56: This locomotive was also built for the McCloud River Railroad. The CWR sold it in 1985 to John Bradley of Willits who planned to use its parts to rebuild Locomotive 53.

No. 57: This locomotive was built for the Southern Pacific.

Nos. 61. 62, and 63: The CWR acquired these locomotives from the Southern Pacific.

M-80: This rail bus was built as a demonstration unit by Mack Trucks, Inc. It was scrapped after being damaged beyond repair in a 1964 collision with Skunk M-100.

M-100: The CWR acquired this rail bus from the Morehead & North Fork Railroad of Kentucky. Its two Buda four-cylinder gasoline engines (each 60-horsepower) were replaced in 1946 with a 150-horsepower Cummins diesel.

M-200: Constructed for the Longview, Portland & Northern Railway and later used by the Trona Railway from which the CWR acquired it in 1941. The original Buda six-cylinder 150-horsepower gasoline engine was replaced in 1955 with a 165-horsepower Cummins diesel. Retired from CWR service January 11, 1975, the rail bus was donated to the Pacific Locomotive Society for use at its Castro Point facility at Richmond, California.

M-300: This rail bus was first used on North Carolina's Aberdeen & Rockfish Railroad. It later served on the Salt Lake, Garfield & Western Railroad's Saltair Route and then sold to the California Western. The CWR replaced the original six-cylinder 168-horsepower Hall-Scott gasoline engine with a 220-horsepower Cummins diesel engine.